Achieving
QTS

Dyslexia-friendly **practice** in the **secondary classroom**

Achieving QTS

Dyslexia-friendly practice in the secondary classroom

Tilly Mortimore and Jane Dupree

LearningMatters

First published in 2008 by Learning Matters Ltd.

British Library Cataloguing in Publication Data
A CIP record for this book is available from the British Library.

ISBN: 978 1 84445 128 9

The rights of Tilly Mortimore and Jane Dupree to be identified as authors of this work has been asserted by them in accordance with the Copyright, Designs and Patents Act 1988.

Cover design by Topics.
Text design by Code 5 Design Associates Ltd.
Project management by Deer Park Productions, Tavistock
Typeset by PDQ Typesetting, Newcastle under Lyme
Printed and bound by Cromwell Press Ltd, Trowbridge, Wiltshire

Learning Matters Ltd
33 Southernhay East
Exeter EX1 1NX
Tel: 01392 215560
info@learningmatters.co.uk
www.learningmatters.co.uk

Contents

The Authors

Tilly Mortimore

Tilly Mortimore is a senior lecturer in Education Studies in the School of Education, Bath Spa University. She taught English and drama in a comprehensive school before setting up English departments in specialist schools for dyslexic learners. She has worked individually with dyslexic students of all ages and provided consultancy support and training for teachers on dyslexia, literacy and learning style in a range of international educational settings including schools and colleges. She completed a PhD and joined the School of Education at Southampton University to lecture on PG MSc courses in dyslexia and inclusion for teacher education. She has published *Dyslexia and learning style: A practitioner's handbook* and articles on dyslexia, learning style, inclusion and support services. She researches in dyslexia, inclusion and vulnerable learners.

Jane Dupree

Jane Dupree is an education consultant who is an experienced trainer and practitioner in the development of literacy skills, thinking skills and study skills. Jane has worked with a wide range of schools delivering in-service training as well as developing programmes for Summer Literacy Schools. She is currently working as a consultant with Dyslexia Action, having previously worked as course director and tutor for those studying for the Post Graduate Diploma in Dyslexia at Masters Level. Jane was responsible for the development of the first Dyslexia Unit within Essex Local Authority for secondary school students, a fully inclusive and successful unit. In 2005 Jane published a practical study skills book, *Help students improve their study skills*. She was part of the development team for the new 6th edition of the highly-respected teaching manual *Alpha to omega* by Bevé Hornsby, published in January 2007. She contributed to the Channel 4 Dyslexia Awareness Week and has written articles for *Dyslexia Contact* on Mind Mapping. In addition, she tutors students using a range of programmes, both from her base in Suffolk and more recently nationwide using interactive video tuition over the internet, as presented in her paper at the 2008 International British Dyslexia Association Conference.

Jane Dupree runs accredited study skills courses using on line learning through her website www.brainwaveseducation.com

Introduction

This book aims to help you to ensure that your classroom and your institution offer the best environment and support for vulnerable learners, such as people with Specific Learning Difficulties (SpLD)/dyslexia. It will offer support in the development of the understanding and skill which will help you to provide strategies appropriate for learners with a range of learning disabilities. However, it is important to appreciate the broader context and climate within which you develop your practice. What is the current understanding of SpLD/dyslexia, disability and inclusion and how does this influence educational practice?

Disability and inclusion

Disability has been defined in Article 14 of the Human Rights Act 1998 as

> a physical or mental impairment which has a substantial and long-term adverse impact on his or her ability to carry out normal day-to-day activities.

People with dyslexia or SpLD are thus considered to have a disability. For centuries throughout the Western world, disability had been placed within a 'medical' framework which depicted it as rooted in the individual's personal biological or cognitive impairments and placed the emphasis upon personal tragedy, with diagnosis by experts and specialised separate facilities. People with disabilities were seen as dependent and different from the 'norm'. The latter years of the twentieth century witnessed radical changes in attitudes towards disability and an attack upon this medical model of disability which was seen as oppressing people with disabilities in that it involved relations of dominance and absence of choice, encouraged discrimination and excluded people from the material benefits of education and society (Barton, 1996).

This challenge, driven by people with disabilities, arose out of the same human rights agenda that achieved equal opportunities for women and ethnic groups in the late twentieth century (Oliver, 1990). It led to the development of a new model of disability, termed the 'social' model, which takes the focus away from the disability, removes the 'problem' from the impaired individual and locates it firmly within the ways in which society establishes physical and conceptual barriers which oppress people with disabilities This social model has radically changed the way in which we expect to work with a range of vulnerable learners and informs much of the thinking in this book. Until comparatively recently, much of the thinking about SpLD/dyslexia arose from the medical model which suggested that responsibility lay with the individual him or herself and with the 'experts' who provided diagnoses and remedies. The social model, however, suggests that we are all responsible for identifying and removing the barriers our classrooms and systems might set in the dyslexic student's pathway, and this spirit informs the concept and development of the inclusive classroom and the 'dyslexia-friendly school' (Mackay, 2004).

The Disability Discrimination Act of 1995 aimed to reduce the social exclusion linked with disability, to ensure social fairness and equal shares for all in the country's resources. The application of the Act to education in 2001 (Special Education Needs and Disability Act –

SENDA) established the right of all students to be educated together in mainstream schools. Inclusion therefore refers to being in an ordinary school with other students following the same curriculum at the same time, in the same classroom, with the full acceptance of everybody involved in the process, and in a way that makes the student feel no different from other students. It is not an easy option. It is not simply a matter of locating a child in a mainstream school and expecting him or her to change and adapt to school life. It is a radical concept which demands we rethink the ways in which the life of the school, teaching and the curriculum is organised and delivered, to create suitable learning support for the whole student population. It affects everyone in the school.

How has inclusion affected teachers?

You are probably aware that inclusion has caused controversy among many groups including parents, policy makers, teachers and learners (Nind, 2005). There is considerable anxiety amongst mainstream classroom teachers, many of whom feel ill-equipped to take on the responsibility of identification and the provision of appropriate support for individuals with specific learning difficulties. Many PGCE students feel anxious that they have received minimal training in special needs. There is, however, one way in which the move from a medical to a social model of disability may help to reduce this fear. The social model of disability emphasises the identification and removal of barriers to learning rather than focusing upon deficits within an individual. Chasty (1985) stated 'If they don't learn the way we teach them, we must teach them the way they learn', and this encourages us to consider how we might identify and adjust those approaches and environments which might cause learners with SpLD/dyslexia to fail. Nind (2005) has suggested that we must move away from a model which focuses upon the 'special' student's need for diagnoses and individualised programmes towards ways of adapting our instructional goals, arrangements, lesson formats, materials, delivery style and classroom environment to help the vulnerable learner to participate successfully. This way our classrooms can become inclusive and the risk of failure be reduced.

Nind suggests that inclusion is a journey and we are all at different stages along the way. Booth and Ainscow published an Index for inclusion (2002) which stresses the need for an inclusive culture – a culture where all are welcome, where staff, students and carers collaborate with each other and where differences are acknowledged and respected. Does this mean that there will be no need for assessment or individualised programmes? This would have theoretical, strategic and financial implications and is contested by those advocates of dyslexia-friendly schools such as Reid (2005) and MacKay (2004), who point out that individual provision for particular learners will remain appropriate. One requirement for gaining dyslexia-friendly school status is the existence on the staff of appropriately trained people who can assess individuals and deliver programmes. This is not, however, the role of the newly qualified teacher.

Establishing a dyslexia-friendly inclusive environment

The aim of this book is to develop your understanding of the strengths and weaknesses experienced by learners with SpLD/dyslexia and the theory that underpins both the suggested dyslexic 'profile' and the types of strategies that might help these learners. It will suggest ways in which you, as a non-specialist subject teacher, can enable dyslexic learners to succeed within your mainstream classroom without placing too heavy a burden upon yourself and to show you how you can introduce these practical measures right from the start of your teaching career. It will take you through a number of activities designed to help you understand and reflect upon the implications of your practice upon everyone within your classroom. Do take the time to share these activities with your colleagues and fellow students – this will help to spread awareness and inclusive attitudes which will contribute to the dyslexia-friendly environment.

With an estimated incidence of between 4 and 10% in the population (Singleton, 1999), dyslexia is arguably one of the most common learning differences that you are likely to encounter in your classroom and therefore it is vital that you should know how to support these learners. The first part of the book explores definitions and theories of SpLD/dyslexia and how these are expressed in behaviours and learning needs. The second part explores the nature of the inclusive classroom, ways in which teachers can develop inclusive teaching practices and the implications for supporting dyslexic learners in the development of appropriate skills across the curriculum. The final part goes beyond the classroom to examine how the school team can co-operate to ensure that the dyslexic learner is supported in a holistic and consistent way.

The Professional Standards

The **Professional Standards for Qualified Teacher Status** include three areas:

1. *Professional attributes* – defined as the attitude, relationships and commitment to practice and development expected of anyone qualifying to be a teacher.

2. *Professional knowledge and understanding* – defined as the authoritative knowledge of the subjects being taught, and understanding of the ways in which the full range of learners should be managed, monitored and assessed.

3. *Professional skills* – defined as the skills involved in planning, delivering, managing and monitoring the development of the whole learner and collaborating with others to ensure a productive learning environment.

The **Core Professional Standards** provide a framework for a teacher's career and clarify how it might progress through maintaining and building on existing professional attributes, knowledge and skills. All the standards are underpinned by the five key outcomes for children and young people identified in *Every Child Matters* (DfES, 2003) and the six areas of the Common Core of skills and knowledge for the children's workforce.

This book aims to support you through the progression from teaching practice to the gaining of Qualified Teacher Status and then through the Induction period, prior to achieving the standards underpinning Core status. As you read, you will realise that all the approaches described relate to many of the standards. The following standards are addressed consistently throughout the book.

Qualified Teacher Status:
Q1, Q3a, Q4, Q5, Q6, Q9, Q14, Q19, Q21b, Q23, Q25, Q28, Q29.

Core:
C1, C3, C4, C5, C6, C9, C14, C19, C27, C28, C29, C30, C31,
(see www.tda.gov.uk/standards)

However, the opening of each chapter will guide you in your understanding of the specific Standards that it covers.

PART 1
WHAT IS DYSLEXIA?

1
Definitions and theories. What is dyslexia?

Chapter objectives

By the end of this chapter you should:
- **have begun to develop a reflexive approach to your activities within the classroom;**
- **be able to justify your choice of the most appropriate approaches for the dyslexia-friendly classroom;**
- **be provided with some research-based answers to these questions.**
  - **What is dyslexia?**
  - **What causes dyslexia?**
  - **How might knowledge gained from research affect what I do in my classroom?**

This chapter addresses the following Professional Standards for QTS and Core:

Q18, C18

Introduction

Most experienced – or hardened – teachers will admit, when pressed, that they struggled through their teaching placement, and often the first year of teaching, living only to sleep and wonder if things would ever get any easier. Luckily for teachers, and for our children, they usually do. Teachers survive and develop skills and strategies which become so automatic that, if asked, they often cannot tell you exactly why their classrooms tick over successfully and how they have managed to avoid conflicts, build relationships and help their students to enjoy their learning. During the first years of the job, however, these skills and strategies need to be spelled out, reflected upon and consciously put into practice. It is challenging enough for a new teacher to deal with the needs of average learners – it is often daunting indeed when you realise that you are also likely to be responsible for the progress and fate of learners with differences such as SpLD/dyslexia and that this responsibility is enshrined within the disability legislation as expressed by the Disability Discrimination Act and the Code of Practice (2001). Before you start to panic, think about how much you know already.

Think about your existing knowledge of SpLD/dyslexia and make a list of your most pressing unanswered questions.

A group of trainee teachers undertaking a special interest study on SpLD/dyslexia came up with the following. No doubt they bear some resemblance to your queries.

Commonly-asked questions about SpLD/dyslexia

- What is dyslexia?
- What causes dyslexia?
- Is dyslexia a middle-class myth?
- How might I spot a learner with dyslexia?
- How many students with dyslexia might I come across in a class?
- How will dyslexia affect my subject?
- How does dyslexia affect a student's behaviour?
- Will I have to teach in a different way?

Dyslexia – controversies and disagreements

You will no doubt be aware that dyslexia is a hotly contested topic. Estimates of incidence in the general population vary from one child in ten (Dyslexia Action, 2007) to the suggestion that dyslexia exists purely as a middle-class myth. There is disagreement over definitions to the extent that Rice and Brooks's (2004) review of dyslexia in adults identified over 70 definitions in current use. There was also controversy over whether the term *specific learning difficulties* or *dyslexia* should be used to describe the pattern of learning differences seen to characterise the syndrome. Dyslexia was the first of the specific learning difficulties to be recognised and the term *specific learning difficulty* historically was often used instead of *dyslexia*. Local Authorities (LAs) have adopted a range of different definitions and, in some LAs, you will still find a reluctance to use terms such as dyslexia, with the more generic term of *SpLD* written on Statements of Special Educational Need (see Chapter 9). However, dyslexia is only one of several specific learning difficulties, with overlapping behavioural characteristics and profiles of strengths and weaknesses that differ. These include dyspraxia and dyscalculia. Since they often present together in a learner, SpLDs are said to be comorbid, that is they can occur together (Deponio, 2004). Chapter 7 provides more information about these.

Historical references to SpLD/dyslexia date from the seventeenth century. The earliest reference to intelligent learners with surprising difficulties in literacy came in 1672 from Thomas Willis, a tutor of young gentlemen (Ott, 1997). In 1877 a German physician, Kussmaul, coined the term 'word-blindness' (Critchley, 1970) and by 1896 the term 'congenital dyslexia' had appeared in a paper published in the Lancet by Pringle-Morgan. This term was linked with Percy F, an exceptionally talented 14 year old mathematician who experienced huge difficulties with reading and writing. James Kerr, Medical Office of Health in Bradford, was simultaneously writing about the children he observed with difficulties in reading and writing but no other cognitive deficits (Pumfrey and Reason, 1991). These two papers laid the foundation for the next one hundred years of research and controversy and set the pattern for the close involvement of the medical world alongside teachers and psychologists. The

British Dyslexia Association and Dyslexia Institute were founded in 1972 and the later years of the twentieth century saw the establishment both of university research departments focusing upon SpLD/dyslexia and a network of Dyslexia Associations around the UK. This did not, however, prevent Professor Julian Elliott from proclaiming the death of dyslexia in 2005. The resulting furore would indicate that this was premature. Why is there so much controversy and disagreement?

There are at least four answers to this.

- It cannot be disputed that we have become an increasingly literacy-based society and that difficulties in this area exclude people from work opportunities and make it more likely that they will suffer from some of the factors associated with poverty. The acquiring of literacy has thus become central to economic survival.
- Another reason (explored further in Chapter 9) is that so much emotion is invested in a 'diagnosis' of dyslexia – failure to learn is highly charged for the learner, the family and the school.
- Another answer is tied in with finance – the notion that a diagnosis of SpLD/dyslexia will open the door to extra support or equipment that is not available to learners with a general learning difficulty. Specialists offer expensive 'cures'. Tensions between a prospective provider attempting to reduce costs and the family of a child threatening to fall through the educational net are almost inevitable.
- Even if it is accepted that a condition which can be defined as 'dyslexia' exists, there is currently no firm consensus as to the underlying causes and there remain areas of disagreement between the researchers within the field. Different causal theories underpin different patterns of behaviour and this must be reflected in differences in definitions of the condition.

How can these dilemmas be resolved for practical classroom teachers? It is highly unlikely, at this stage in your career, that you will be expected to get involved in 'diagnosing' dyslexia – you are not qualified to do so and you should refer any suggestions of this type to the Special Educational Needs Co-ordinator (SENCo) and to your mentor. You will however have two priorities. It **is** your role to be aware of the types of learning profile associated with dyslexic differences so that you can spot these students, support them appropriately, and refer them on to the SENCo for advice or, if needed, further specialist assessment. You will also want to offer the best possible support for individual vulnerable learners to enable them to make the most of their time in school, to utilise their areas of strength to compensate for the things they find hard and to prevent them from disrupting your classroom. To enable you to do both these things – to identify and support learners with dyslexic type differences – you need to clarify your understanding of the following things.

- How will you define SpLD/ dyslexia?
- What are the learning differences that accompany SpLD/dyslexia?
- What are the casual theories underpinning SpLD/dyslexia?

Defining dyslexia

The SpLD/ dyslexia world involves a broad range of stakeholders – there are learners with dyslexia, families, teachers, school governors, educational psychologists, specialist thera-pists, researchers, educational policy makers and academics. Each has his or her own agenda, context and needs. This will influence the type of definition each adopts. You are currently a mainstream secondary school teacher. Your chosen definition will need to enable you to focus upon a particular learning profile and to adjust your activities and classroom to support this. It will also need to be clear enough for you to explain to others. What definition might you choose?

PRACTICAL TASK PRACTICAL TASK **PRACTICAL TASK** PRACTICAL TASK **PRACTICAL TASK**

Write a brief definition of SpLD/ dyslexia as you understand it.

Now turn to Appendix 1. You will find a series of definitions of SpLD/ dyslexia. Read them and consider how each is influenced by its context. Are there any that seem particularly relevant to you? Record the number.

The remainder of this chapter explores the research that underpins the various definitions provided and suggests a comprehensive definition. For the time being your definition of SpLD/dyslexia is likely to be based upon your understanding of how dyslexia affects the individual. There are, however, a number of myths surrounding dyslexia and some of these may be affecting your understanding. It is therefore important to establish how many of these have been verified by research.

How many of the following statements are true? Place **T** for *true*; **M** for *myth* and **S** for *sometimes* in column 2 and then check in Appendix 1 to see how accurate your understanding is. Correct any mistakes in column 3.

SpLD/dyslexia statement	T/M/S
1. The majority of dyslexic learners are male.	
2. Dyslexic individuals are usually good at art.	
3. Dyslexic learners will never learn to read.	
4. Dyslexia runs in families.	
5. Dyslexia does not exist in other languages.	
6. Dyslexic learners have difficulty with mathematics.	
7. Most dyslexic learners suffer from attention disorders.	
8. All dyslexic individuals are disorganised.	
9. Dyslexic individuals are usually good at sport.	
10. Dyslexic learners need to put extra effort into their school work.	
11. Dyslexic children have difficulty concentrating.	
12. Dyslexic learners are articulate.	
13. Dyslexic children often have difficulties with their peer group.	
14. Dyslexic learners have low self-esteem.	
15. Many dyslexic learners have difficulty with alphabetical order.	
16. It is impossible to identify dyslexia before the age of 7.	
17. Brain activity in language processing differs between those with and without SpLD.	
18. Dyslexic learners are highly creative.	

19. Dyslexic students find it hard to express themselves in writing.	
20. Dyslexia does not exist.	
21. All dyslexic learners are of average or above average intelligence.	
22. Dyslexic learners cannot cope at university.	
23. Dyslexic children are impulsive.	
24. Dyslexic learners have trouble listening to information.	
25. There is more than one type of dyslexia.	
26. Dyslexic learners are all likely to have right-brain thought characteristics.	
27. Dyslexic learners have trouble with eye-strain.	
28. Dyslexic learners have difficulty with short-term memory.	
29. Dyslexic learners are clumsy.	
30. Dyslexic learners have persistent difficulties with spelling.	
31. Dyslexic learners have trouble with lists and sequences.	
32. Dyslexic learners have trouble focussing on more than one activity at a time.	
33. Dyslexic learners find it hard to make skills automatic.	
34. Dyslexic learners suffer from early language delay.	
35. Dyslexic learners have more difficulty than most with taking notes.	
36. Dyslexic learners find it hard to copy from a board.	
37. Dyslexic learners have poor letter formation and written presentation.	
38. Dyslexic learners have difficulty with articulation.	
39. A dyslexic learner will be the class clown.	
40. Dyslexic learners produce mirror writing.	
41. Dyslexic adults will read slowly and laboriously.	
42. Dyslexic learners are usually left-handed.	
43. Dyslexic learners have low reading ages and high IQs.	
44. Dyslexic learners always come from middle-class families.	

How knowledgeable are you? You will see that there are nine 'myths'. Part one of this book explores and explains the implications of all these statements in more depth. Experience and research do indeed disprove the nine myths and indicate that there are certain 'truths': SpLD/dyslexia does run in families (Stein, 2007); there do seem to be differences in brain processing during reading and language processing between individuals with and without dyslexia (Bruck, 1992); there does seem to be more than one type of dyslexia, or at least differing profiles of strength and weakness. It is also reported consistently (Klein, 1995; Riddick, 1996; Reid, 2003;) that learners with dyslexia are more than likely to display indicators of dyslexic type differences and that these will persist into adulthood (Frith, 1997; Mortimore and Crozier, 2006).

The following are indicators of dyslexic type differences.

1. Difficulties with formulating and following lists and sequences.
2. Difficulties with short-term memory and organisation.
3. Difficulties with written expression and planning.
4. Difficulties taking notes.

5. Difficulties copying.
6. Persistent difficulties with spelling.
7. Difficulties automatising skills.
8. Extra effort will be required with school/college work.
9. Adults will read laboriously – reading difficulties persist – even if well compensated.

You will, however, notice that the majority (23) of the Dyslexia *Truth, Myth* or *Sometimes* statements fall into the '*Sometimes*' category. This is crucial to your understanding of people with dyslexia. Each is an individual with his or her own profile of strength and weakness. If one of your students is consistently exhibiting the indicators above, he or she may also have trouble with some of the '*sometimes*' factors. However, this is not necessarily the case and this is where you must avoid stereotyping and must develop ways of investigating further. Chapters 2 and 3 discuss the types of behaviour that might indicate dyslexic type differences and also provide you with some ideas as to how to compile a profile to inform the ways in which you can support the student within your subject.

These nine indicators for dyslexia have emerged from research into the behaviour and experiences of students with SpLD/dyslexia at a range of stages in their education. How might they link with the research into the underlying causes of dyslexia?

RESEARCH SUMMARY RESEARCH SUMMARY **RESEARCH SUMMARY** RESEARCH SUMMARY

Causal theories of dyslexia

What causes dyslexia?

Prior to the 1980s the main source of information about SpLD/dyslexia was the observation of behaviours, for example the sub-skills of reading. The development, however, of ways of investigating the brain activity which underpins these behaviours has begun to offer the possibility of a more detailed understanding of SpLD/dyslexia, although there is still a long way to go before we can be really confident of our facts (Rice and Brooks, 2004).

The 1980s and 1990s resounded with clashes between academics, neuroscientists and psychologists investigating the reading process which continues to exert a strong influence over research into dyslexia. Three major competing causal theories of SpLD/dyslexia emerged. If you wish to examine these in more detail, Reid and Wearmouth (2002) present chapters from each perspective. They comprise the following.

1. The phonological deficit theory.
2. The magnocellular deficit hypothesis.
3. The cerebellar deficit hypothesis.

The phonological deficit theory

This has been the most influential theory over the past thirty years. What is a phonological deficit? This does not refer a person's capacity to hear sound at the physical level but to the ability to process phonemes, or sounds within words at the cognitive level. People who hear perfectly well can experience difficulty when required to identify, sequence and reproduce sounds within a word (see Snowling 2000 for further details). It has been suggested that these phonological difficulties emerge from abnormalities in the language areas in the brain which persist throughout life. This could explain why dyslexic adults who have learnt to read still exhibit abnormal brain activity while reading (Bruck, 1992; Rack, 1994).

The studies of Snowling (2000), Stanovich (1988) and others suggested that people with dyslexia show a selective deficiency in the ability to process the sounds of their native language despite other aspects of their language, such as vocabulary and expressive language skills, remaining normal. They explain that normal reading and spelling develops successfully because children map the speech sounds they hear on to the speech sounds they produce, and vice versa, to create what Snowling and Hulme (1994) termed 'phono-logical representations' in their memory. The representations created by children with dyslexia are fuzzier and less finely detailed than those of other children. Thus speech and phonological ability are crucial both to the development of literacy and the nature of dyslexic deficits. Hatcher and Snowling (2002) suggest that the severity of these phonological proces-sing difficulties will reduce the types of strategies that an affected learner can use to develop reading and spelling skills and therefore dictate the nature of that child's reading and spelling development. Chapter 2 will explore the effect these difficulties might have upon a student's behaviour. These fuzzy representations also cause difficulties for verbal short term memory where the memory traces of dyslexic learners are less clear. Pickering (2004) suggested that inefficient short term memory is one of the basic causal factors of SpLD/dyslexia.

This phonological deficit theory was dominant and was embellished by further research findings such as those of Denckla and Rudel (1976), Tallal (1984) and Wolf and Bowers (2000). They were interested in the speed with which individuals process different elements of language and they identified a particularly disadvantaged group of individuals who were not only inaccurate in their phonological processing but also suffered from deficits in proces-sing speed, fluency or naming-speed. This became known as the 'double-deficit hypothesis'.

The magnocellular deficit theory

The phonological deficit hypothesis remained the core explanation and has underpinned the strategies offered for developing literacy in children with SpLD/dyslexia. However, most of these researchers were academics who did not work on a daily basis with dyslexic learners and not everyone was convinced that a phonological processing difficulty could explain all of the differences, strengths and weaknesses they observed in their work with students (Mortimore, 2003). There had been some suggestion during the 1980s and early 1990s that visual deficits might play a role. In 1997, Stein and Walsh (1997) suggested that a sensory defect in the large nerve cells in the eye, known as 'magnocells' might be a cause of dyslexia. These cells occur within the pathway between the retina and the visual cortex of the brain. They carry information about rapid movement or changes within the environment and, should defects in these cause images to be unstable, this will reduce the efficiency of processing print or symbols. This also can contribute to eye-strain, headaches and ability to concentrate upon print. The emergence of this second theory, which seemed to link with the experiences of some individuals with dyslexic type reading difficulties that were not explained by the phonological deficit theory, led to suggestions that there might be subtypes of dyslexia which manifest in different ways (Robertson and Bakker, 2002). The magnocellular theory suggested the need to include a type of reading support strategy which emphasised the development of visual processing skills as well as the phonological. It did not, however, challenge the phonological deficit theory in any significant way.

The cerebellar deficit hypothesis

This was not the case with the emergence of the work of Nicolson and Fawcett in the late eighties which gave rise to a broadening of the approach to dyslexia research, diagnosis and support but also a storm of controversy. They reported on a study (Nicolson and Fawcett, 1994) which compared school students with and without SpLD/dyslexia. The dyslexic group revealed severe deficits in balance, motor skill, phonological skill and rapid processing when compared with the controls. Nicolson and Fawcett claimed that this was caused by deficits within the cerebellum.

The cerebellum is placed at the back of the brain and is sometimes termed the hind brain. Independent limb movements and especially those requiring rapid skills are managed by the cerebellum. Nicolson (2002) used Positron Emission Tomography (PET) brain scan findings from the 1990s to support the significance of the cerebellum in the acquisition and use of a range of cognitive skills including using language fluently, skill automatisation and balance. Nicolson and Fawcett and a range of other research groups carried out a number of studies between 2001 and 2004 and claimed that those difficulties suffered by dyslexic children could be attributed to cerebellar abnormality.

This theory was not accepted by the majority of researchers, remains controversial and speculative and has been further complicated by its links with the difficulties accompanying the claims of the DDAT programme of activities. It did, however, offer a unifying causal framework or explanation for some of the difficulties observed in dyslexia such as phonological processing, central processing speed, motor skills, and difficulties making skills automatic, all of which can be linked with deficits in cerebellar processing.

A current consensus?

So what is the current situation and how does it help us to define SpLD/dyslexia? It is fair to say that for some years, there was little harmony or agreement. However, things have moved on, helped by a combination of research developments and changes in thinking. On the research front, Stein's earlier studies into the role of magnocellular neurones in the development of dyslexia originally seemed purely to refer to visual processing. He had already estimated that over 20% of differences in reading ability, based on orthography or visual properties of language, could be explained by visual magnocellular sensitivity because difficulty stabilising letters in the mind's eye undermines and slows down phonological skills and processing. He has now (2007) moved on to propose that the visual magnocellular system is linked to phonological processing and that these magnocellular neurones are also involved in determining the levels of sensitivity to the changes in sound which are required to distinguish between phonemes such as 'm' and 'n'. Thus a faulty auditory magnocellular system further undermines phonological processing. He also suggests that the magnocellular system has a significant part to play in communicating with the cerebellum, which he terms the 'brain's autopilot' (Stein, 2007). These findings suggest that the magnocellular neuronal systems of the brain underpin auditory, visual and motor temporal elements of speech and reading. This means that they will play a strong part in all aspects of literacy, co-ordination and the development of automaticity and can be seen as an underlying causal factor which might cut across the three causal theories previously accepted without destroying any of them.

In 1999, Frith played a significant part in reconciling the tensions between the three theories when she devised her causal models of dyslexia (described in Frith, 2002). She insisted that there must be three levels of description to provide a complete explanation of any developmental disorder. At the most basic level lies the biological or brain system where causes or possible deficits exist within the neurological framework or architecture of the brain. At the most superficial level we can observe behaviours and can speculate as to what causes them. In between these two levels lies the cognitive layer, where thought processing occurs, which connects the behaviours we can observe to the biological or brain systems which have influenced their development. All three levels are of course affected by, and interact with, an individual's environmental context, which in its turn can shape the brain architecture (Blakemore and Frith, 2005).

Returning to research, developments in neuro-psychological techniques are now beginning to reveal the brain architecture and processing that underpins both the cognitive and behavioural levels. The large number of factors involved and the role played by the environment means that similar deficits in brain function at the biological level might affect cognitive processes and behaviours in different ways across different individuals.

The past ten years has also seen huge developments in research into genetic markers for dyslexia (Knight and Hynd, 2002). Stein has been involved in research attempting to identify genes which might be implicated in the development of dyslexia and of conditions such as dyspraxia, ADHD and autism which can sometimes co-exist with dyslexia. Again, it is early days but interest has been caught by genes located on Chromosome 6 and these may show links between dyslexia and many of the immunity anomalies sometimes observed in individuals with dyslexia.

There therefore seems to have been a softening of the attitudes of opposing theorists, perhaps the feeling that these differing sets of behaviours or 'symptoms' may well be connected in ways that can be revealed by further research into aspects of the architecture of the brain which can underpin them all. Fawcett (2004) expressed this as an allegory drawn from a Hindu story about an elephant and three blindfolded people – maybe they are researchers – the researcher at the back of the animal describes the elephant as a little stringy rope, the one in the middle talks of high hairy walls and the one at the front says it is a python. Only when the blindfolds come off do they realise the truth.

So, what is dyslexia?

How does this discussion of causal theory help us to establish our definition of SpLD/dyslexia? An understanding of how this research has helped the evolution of a definition of dyslexia is an essential prerequisite to this. It will enable us to determine where difficulties and learning differences might emerge, what might underpin them and enable us to provide explanations and information for those who need it. Look again at the definitions provided in the appendix and think about the one you selected. Are you still happy to take it as a working definition? You will need to revisit it at various stages through this first section of the book as your understanding of the syndrome, and of your role, grows.

The definitions change over time in response to context and research findings and have highlighted mainly the deficits associated with SpLD/dyslexia since, as a teacher, the learners you come across are likely to be attempting to deal with classroom demands which highlight their most vulnerable areas of processing and therefore will be seeing their dyslexia as a liability. We will examine later many of the individual strengths that dyslexic learners can bring, and explore whether conceptualising dyslexia in terms of deficits and difficulties is necessarily helpful. For you as a teacher, arguably the most important demand is to be aware of the profile of cognitive strengths and weaknesses you might expect in a learner with dyslexic differences and how to offer the type of support that makes learning accessible.

Frith's definition (2002) is based upon deficits, but does seem to bring together the different elements of dyslexia evident throughout the research literature.

> *The consensus is emerging that dyslexia is a neuro-developmental disorder with a biological origin, which impacts on speech processing with a range of clinical manifestations. There is evidence for a genetic basis and there is evidence for a brain basis, and it is clear that the behavioural signs extend well beyond written language. There may be many different kinds of genes and different kinds of brain conditions that are ultimately responsible for the dyslexia syndrome, but in each case the symptoms have to be understood within the relevant cultural context.*
>
> (2002, p65)

This is very much a researcher's definition. The current Dyslexia Action definition might perhaps be more useful to you in your classroom. How does it fit with the definition you chose? Can you justify your choice? Will you stick with it?

> *Dyslexia is a specific learning difficulty that mainly affects reading and spelling. Dyslexia is characterised by difficulties in processing word-sounds and by weaknesses in short-term verbal memory; its effects may be seen in spoken language as well as written language. The current evidence suggests that these difficulties arise from inefficiencies in language-processing areas in the left hemisphere of the brain which, in turn, appear to be linked to genetic differences.*
>
> *Dyslexia is life-long, but its effects can be minimised by targeted literacy intervention, technological support and adaptations to ways of working and learning. Dyslexia is not related to intelligence, race or social background. Dyslexia varies in severity and often occurs alongside other specific learning difficulties, such as Dyspraxia or Attention Deficit Disorder, resulting in variation in the degree and nature of individuals' strengths and weaknesses.*
>
> (Dyslexia Action (formerly Dyslexia Institute) 25.07.2007)

A SUMMARY OF **KEY POINTS**

> There are many controversies around definitions and causal theories of dyslexia.

> There are three major causal theories, formerly in competition.

> Frith's model provides a way of understanding how these theories may not necessarily be contradictory but simply reflect the ways that SpLD/dyslexia manifests at three different levels – the behavioural, cognitive and biological.

> SpLD/dyslexia can be seen as a 'pattern of differences' in learning (Miles, 1983).

> Each learner's profile will be individual but is likely to reflect this pattern of differences.

MOVING *ON* > > > > > > MOVING *ON* > > > > > > MOVING *ON*

The next stage is to use your growing understanding of the nature of dyslexia, and the research base that underpins it, to discuss the types of behaviours that you might observe in a classroom and how you might begin to use them to establish the most effective support.

REFLECTIVE TASK

Suggest two concepts, ideas, suggestions from this chapter that are already part of your current teaching ASK (attributes, skills, knowledge).

Select one new suggestion from the chapter and review and reflect on its implications for your teaching.

FURTHER READING FURTHER READING FURTHER READING FURTHER READING

Thomson, M (2001) *The psychology of dyslexia*. London: Whurr.

Ott, P (2007) *Teaching children with dyslexia. A practical guide*. Abingdon: Routledge.

Reid, G (2006) *Dyslexia.* The SEN Series. London: Continuum.

Pumfrey, P D and Reason, R (1998) *Specific learning difficulties (dyslexia): Challenges and responses*. Abingdon and New York: RoutledgeFalmer.

Reid, G (2003) *Dyslexia, A practitioner's handbook*. 3rd edition. Chichester: Wiley.

Reid, G and Wearmouth, J (2002) (eds) *Dyslexia and literacy*. Chichester: Wiley.

Snowling, M J (2000) *Dyslexia.* 2nd edition. Oxford: Blackwell.

Turner, M and Rack, J (2004) *The study of dyslexia*. New York: Kluwer Academic/Phenum.

To follow the arguments as to causal theories in more depth, you are recommended to follow up Reid and Wearmouth (2002) or Turner and Rack (2004)

2
Behaviours – what might you notice?

Chapter objectives

By the end of this chapter you should:

- **know how the knowledge of definitions and theory that you have gained from Chapter 1 could help you to spot differences before they become difficulties;**
- **be able to analyse the tasks that you set your students to discover which elements might prove excessively difficult for students with SpLD/dyslexia.**

This chapter addresses the following Professional Standards for QTS and Core:

Q2, C2

A major aim of this book is to help you build bridges effectively so as to prevent small misunderstandings becoming major breakdowns. So, what clues might you pick up from your students?

Introduction

Chapter 1 defined dyslexia and discussed some of the theories that attempt to explain the pattern of differences underpinning the syndrome. What is more likely to be important to you, however, is what happens in your classroom. Acceptable or disruptive behaviour can make or break both lessons and relationships between learners, peers and teachers and can encourage or prevent learning for everyone in the classroom. Here are some comments from adults with dyslexia remembering things they tried to cope with at school.

> *Imagine what it's like thinking of a new excuse every day to get out of reading in class. EVERY DAY for ten years plus. I got slung out of school eventually. I was told to read just once too often, then someone laughed when I couldn't pronounce things right and I lost it. Thumped him, threw stuff, threatened the teacher. It was sort of downhill from there. Never did get my GCSEs.*
>
> Tony, lorry driver and mature student

> *My teacher used to give us lists of spellings every week to learn for the test. My Mum and I started out working really hard on them. We'd spend ages. Some weeks I'd do fine – others I couldn't get more than a couple right. My teacher made me stay in at break those days because she said I hadn't done my homework. That meant I couldn't run around and got all twitchy in the lesson after. That often meant I had to stay in at lunchtime too. By afternoon school I was climbing the walls. In the end I stopped going on spelling test days.*
>
> Gina, charity fund raiser

> *From the day I started school to the day I finished, I hated every minute except at art or PE. Teachers can be the most evil of people – pent-up hatred, fickle or no*

time. I was in remedial for English, top band for maths.... I'm not so ashamed now. It's been a hell of a journey going through finding out I was dyslexic. But at last I felt at liberty to be myself – I didn't feel stupid any more. It's horrible from a child onwards being told you're stupid. Some of the teachers were awful – they'd read out spellings in front of the class and humiliate me.... I've got butterflies in the stomach now [just talking about this].... I have the right to support in dealing with it – I don't like asking for support and I know it will be there now – she's not condescending – you don't need another school teacher.

JD, mature art student

I was really good at the science – I understood it all and loved the experiments. When it came to writing it up, however, I was hopeless. My stuff used to come back with red ink all over it. Comments like 'Must try harder', 'Check your spelling'. I only wish I could! At least I can stop Stevie from feeling the way I did.

Stacey, mother of dyslexic son

These adults are typical of learners with dyslexia who dropped out of school as a result of the lack of understanding and support they received. They were looking back on their school days across the space of twenty years, yet these memories are still as raw as when they were laid down. Edwards (1994) provides a stark picture of the effect of the negative experiences of a group of learners with dyslexia. Much has changed since the 1970s and 80s when they were at school. However, children in today's classrooms still tell similar stories and the incidence of illiteracy amongst young people in youth custody remains shockingly high. Many of these young people spend parts of their adult lives in prison; a proportion of them suffer from dyslexia and those who work with dyslexic adults still hear accounts of misunderstandings and opportunities lost from those who are now trying to take up study or improve their job prospects.

If you read through the four stories, you will see that they contain pivotal moments when the teacher might have understood why the individual was behaving in ways that seemed so irritating, that he or she might have responded differently and, as a result, have built bridges which could have supported these students in their learning rather than alienating them and generating long-lasting defensive barriers.

REFLECTIVE TASK

Revising the theory

What were the three main causal theories for SpLD/dyslexia discussed in the previous chapter?

What cognitive processing differences or difficulties with learning might be linked with each of these theories?

When you have completed this, check the section headed Dyslexic differences and challenging tasks on page 21 of this chapter where you will find a list of the types of difficulty or difference that accompany SpLD/ dyslexia. You will find that many of these learning differences could be linked to more than one of these causal theories. You should also remember that SpLD/dyslexia has been termed a syndrome or a 'pattern of differences' (Miles, 1983) and that individuals will display different profiles according to their particular pattern of strengths and weaknesses.

The next stage is to consider how these cognitive processing differences might be expressed in the sort of behaviours that you might notice within your classroom.

Consider these three case studies.

CASE STUDY
Laura (aged 14)
Laura usually sits near the front of the class. She is a potential rebel, fascinated by green issues, the environment, the threats posed by pollution and global warming and corporate greed. In the class discussion she is clear and articulate, makes frequent comments that are both original and apt. In the group work following the class introduction, she discusses eagerly with her friends as they all collect and evaluate ideas for a written presentation to be compiled as homework. Next day she hands in half a side of untidy unsophisticated work. When you challenge her, she is defiant. 'Didn't have time' she says. Another after-school detention for uncompleted work.

CASE STUDY
Peto (aged 15)
Peto always sits at the back of the class in that corner of the room that erupts into counter-culture chat if you aren't watching them. His legs stick out ready to trip up the unwary. His shirt is hanging out; forget the tie. The miscellaneous contents of his back-pack are scattered across his desk but don't seem to include a usable pen. He always seems to be doodling, dreaming or sleeping when he should be following the information you are giving to the class, but from time to time he says something which proves he has picked up and understood what you are talking about. How much does he take in? Difficult to estimate since written work and homework do not play much part in his repertoire.

CASE STUDY
Denny (aged 12)
Denny always sits at the very edge of everything. You have already been concerned by him because he says so little and it seems that other students pick on him and sometimes reduce him to lashing out at them. You have to drag written work out of him and he sometimes rips it up before you can save it. From time to time his pen will suddenly cover him with ink or he'll hit the child next to him or do that one thing you have expressly forbidden the class to do. This means he has to leave the room. This often coincides with a point at which students are being expected to read text around the room or explain a point to the rest of the group. He doesn't seem to mind being sent out of the room.

Do any of these students have dyslexia or specific learning difficulties? Laura is articulate, thoughtful but seems to have major difficulties with written presentation. She seems at first glance to be a stereotypical 'dyslexic learner' – despite the fact that she is a girl and, for many years, the ratio of girls to boys was considered to be around 1 to 4 (Miles et al., 1998). Recent research (Shaywitz et al., 1990; Stein, 2004) questions this imbalance suggesting that it has more to do with the nature of assessment and the different ways in which boys and girls might respond to dyslexic differences than to the impact of gender upon processing skills. However, Laura could just have better things to do with her time over the weekend than homework. Does she have problems at home? Has she been partying all weekend? Is she just stroppy and can't be bothered when she actually has to do some work, or is she severely dyslexic and unable to express herself on paper despite obvious ability? It is not easy to decide.

What about Peto – is he a potentially clever dyslexic student whose negative experiences, when he encountered severe literacy difficulties in primary school, have led him to choose to avoid failure and ridicule and impress his peers by joining the 'cool' guys, acting class clown and causing trouble? He could, of course, simply be one of those frustrating able boys who have chosen to opt out of school when they hit adolescence.

And then Denny. Is his silence due to problems relating to his peers? Is it down to all-round mild learning difficulties? Unidentified speech and language deficits, in which case he cannot be dyslexic because dyslexic learners don't have language difficulties, do they? Or is he a virtual non-reader due to unidentified dyslexia who is concealing his difficulties? Denny is even harder to assess as his limited language use means that he does not shine orally.

Any one of these students might or might not have dyslexia. It is clear that it is not particularly easy to identify dyslexia in students from their behaviour. There is also a question as to how necessary it is to identify dyslexia in any particular learner. Chapter 3 will explore the role played by assessment and diagnosis in an inclusive setting, while the current chapter discusses ways in which a classroom teacher might be able to identify the type of profile linked with SpLD/dyslexia which might indicate a need for further investigation by specialist teachers or the SENCo. We would argue, however, that this type of profiling is not relevant only to vulnerable learners such as those with SpLD/dyslexia. Each learner, with or without dyslexia, will have strengths, weaknesses and preferences in these processing skills and it is therefore general good teaching to be aware of the needs of all your learners and the demands that you are making of them.

So what information do we gain from looking at Laura, Peto and Denny? Firstly we become aware that it is not easy to spot those with dyslexic differences and that overlooking the possibility of dyslexia causes misunderstandings and lasting unhappiness. We should also notice that two of these learners exhibit unexpected difficulties with literacy when their overall ability and use of language is taken into account. This sense of unexpected deficits in a profile which is otherwise of at least average ability is something which experienced practitioners frequently refer to, despite the fact that what has been termed a 'deficit definition' has been heavily criticised by researchers and psychologists on a number of grounds (Reid, 2003) and should be treated with caution. Students whose cognitive skills seem more limited can also experience the difficulties associated with dyslexia (Stanovich, 1996). However, as a classroom teacher, you are likely to be more struck by those learners who show discrepancies between spoken and written expression or those with a gap between the listening comprehension and decoding of a written text. These students with specific learning difficulties just strike you as different from students who have difficulties across the whole range of cognitive areas involved in learning.

This should not mean that you discount the possibility of dyslexic type differences in a student like Denny, who may also be struggling with speech and language difficulties which mask his skills in non-verbal activities. Snowling and Stackhouse (2006) emphasise that a sizeable cohort of students assessed as having SpLD/dyslexia also experience difficulties with language which makes their dyslexia more difficult to spot and will also mean that they need support with the development of both receptive and expressive language skills.

SpLD/dyslexia has been presented in mainly negative terms so far. This is because you are likely to be in a situation where it is the negative side of the syndrome which is causing hardship to the learner, and to you as teacher, and you need to be aware of the reasons for making the adjustments to your classroom and your teaching suggested in this book. Many students with SpLD/dyslexia have striking talents in a range of areas including lateral thinking, imagination, artistic and technical skills, construction, sport, music, architecture, science, mathematics, business, acting, writing. Those adults with SpLD who have succeeded in their chosen fields also show remarkable qualities of perseverance and adaptability in the ways in which they have structured their lives to overcome any disadvantages that their processing differences might have posed. What do the following people have in common?

Richard Branson	August Rodin
Albert Einstein	Jamie Oliver
Richard Rogers	Steven Redgrave
Benjamin Zephaniah	Eddie Izzard
Kiera Knightley	Winston Churchill
Tom Cruise	Oliver Reed
Whoopi Goldberg	Bob Hoskins
Gustav Flaubert	W.B. Yeats
Agatha Christie	

Source: www.dyslexia-test.com/famous.html

You have no doubt guessed it. They have all either talked publicly about their dyslexia or, if born prior to our current understanding of SpLD/dyslexia, were reported to have experienced extreme difficulty with literacy or the written word. Agatha Christie wrote of herself:

> *Writing and spelling were always terribly difficult for me. My letters were without originality. I was an extraordinary bad speller and have remained so until this day.*

Gustav Flaubert, author *Madame Bovary*, according to his niece:

> *Having made a strenuous effort to understand the symbols he could make nothing of, he wept giant tears ... For a long time he could not understand the elementary connection that made of two letters one syllable, of several syllables a word.*

SpLD/dyslexia should not be allowed to be a barrier to talent. However, it is also important to realise that there is no evidence that dyslexia alone brings with it any particular gift or specific ways of thinking that might distinguish dyslexic individuals from their peers (Mortimore, 2008).

So how might these cognitive processing or physiologically based differences affect the behaviour that you notice in the classroom?

Dyslexic differences and challenging tasks

This is a list of the types of processing difficulties experienced by learners and recorded by teachers, students, parents and researchers.

1. **Literacy development**:
a. difficulty in repeating multi-syllabic words;
b. poor phonological awareness (discrimination of speech sounds) or awareness of rhyme and stress within words;
c. cannot identify the constituent sounds in spoken words;
d. difficulty in mapping sounds (phonemes) onto letter symbols (graphemes) expressed in spelling difficulties and strategies;
e. difficulty in learning the letters of the alphabet and alphabetic systems;
f. difficulty with note-taking;
g. loses place when reading;
h. literacy skills lag behind overall performance and apparent ability;
i. difficulty learning everyday sequences e.g. days of week, months of year and multiplication tables;
j. the child has difficulty in retaining and retrieving technical language e.g. mathematical terms.

2. **Behaviour**:
a. poor attention span, easily distracted;
b. embarrassed by apparent difficulties;
c. becoming alienated from his or her peers, becoming isolated, tending to work/play alone;
d. denying difficulties or rejecting help;
e. appearing depressed;
f. becoming the 'class clown';
g. becoming uncharacteristically aggressive;
h. complaining of headaches or 'itchy' eyes when reading;
i. using range of 'distracting' techniques to avoid starting to write/read;
j. difficulties completing tasks, accessing information/words, under time pressure;
k. needs unexpected extra time to complete tasks;
l. difficulty doing more than one thing at a time.

3. **Organisational and motor skills**:
a. untidy, illegible, incorrectly-formed, reversed or disproportionately sized letters or words when handwriting;
b. an awkward position for writing (close to the page/head tilted). Sometimes difficulty with tasks involving fine motor skills;
c. inability to keep within the lines when writing or colouring;
d. difficulty in structuring written work;
e. difficulty copying from the board and textbooks;
f. little idea of time or the structure of the daily timetable;
g. consistently forgets pens, pencils, P.E. kit, letters home, arrangements, etc;
h. difficulty following instructions/directions – frequently getting lost, arriving late.

4. Memory:
a. difficulty following sets of instructions;
b. short-term memory difficulties;
c. difficulty with any type of rote learning.

It is important to remember that each learner is an individual and will not exhibit all of these traits or processing differences. As you know, dyslexia is one of the range of specific learning difficulties which include dyscalculia, dyspraxia, Attention Deficit Disorder/Attention Deficit Hyperactivity Disorder (ADD or ADHD), Asperger's Syndrome and speech and language disorders. Each of these can co-exist with dyslexia and some individuals will exhibit patterns of complex needs which should be brought to the attention of the SENCo and your mentor. Chapter 5 will explore the impact of dyspraxia and dyscalculia. For those of you interested in other learning differences, suggested reading is provided in the recommended reading at the end of this chapter.

How might these behaviours or difficulties with processing skills affect life in school? The pressures upon teachers mean that there is frequently little time to think carefully about the demands any task is making on the learner. For those of us who find most academic tasks easy, it can be salutary when we attempt to break a school-based task down into its components and to examine exactly how many sub-skills need to be in place to enable our students to complete it. One aspect of processing affected by SpLD/dyslexia is automaticity – or the way in which certain sub-skills become so automatic and take up so little processing space or effort that we do not notice ourselves doing them. The cerebellar deficit hypothesis suggests that automaticity is reduced in individuals with SpLD/dyslexia who therefore consistently use far more concentration and processing space than those without dyslexia when undertaking complex skills. An example would be decoding words where the ability simultaneously to decode and comprehend or infer is compromised. You may well find that some of the difficulties your students are experiencing are implicit in the nature of the task you are setting them, which may well be reflected in their responses to it and to you.

You will find it helpful to familiarise yourself with the dyslexic cognitive processing difficulties above and to keep them in mind while you carry out the following activity.

PRACTICAL TASK PRACTICAL TASK **PRACTICAL TASK** PRACTICAL TASK **PRACTICAL TASK**

What are the processing demands posed by a typical task that you expect your students to do?

Select one task that you regularly ask your students to do. It can be anything from expecting them to fill in their homework diaries, complete a mathematical problem, discuss a topic in a group, learn a list of dates, etc.

Look at the list of processing difficulties and list the ones that might affect a student's ability to complete the task.

Discuss your list with a colleague, your mentor or the SENCo, where available.

You will need to consider the demands posed by all the important tasks you set.

How might you notice this Pattern of Difficulties?

Dyslexic differences in the classroom

SpLD/dyslexia has an impact on all the following skills:

1. memory;
2. phonological development;
3. sequencing;
4. processing speed;
5. automaticity;
6. organisation;
7. orientation;
8. numeracy.

These all have a knock-on effect upon self-esteem and confidence, which, in turn, affects social skills and classroom behaviour.

Establishing the profile of a vulnerable or challenging student and then teaching to strengths while compensating for weaknesses is not only appropriate for students with SpLD/dyslexia but will help you to support and include the whole range of vulnerable learners. It may seem time consuming initially but is only likely to be necessary for a small number of learners and the attention, time and stress saved later by the prevention of challenging behaviour and failure will reward you. It is usually the case that behaviour management difficulties stem from a very small group of individuals and then spread to others. If you can ensure that these students are not simply behaving badly in response to teaching that does not match their needs, you are likely to reduce difficult behaviour to a small core with specific primary problems with behaviour, or even to eliminate it.

CASE STUDY
Tom: Year 9

A year 9 group were taken on a history trip to World War I battlefields. Tom was only just allowed to come and arrived with a record sheet labelling him with ADHD and which described a number of incidents where he had run out of classes, been rude, refused to do work and had been termed 'unteachable' by members of staff. None of the staff on the trip had previously taught him. He was 'buzzy', tense and defensive on the journey and sat with a small group of boys who also had records of difficult behaviour. When staff responded to them all calmly and with humour, Tom relaxed and became fascinated by everything he saw, asking many questions and obviously relishing the positive attention offered. When required to fill out a work book and to talk about his findings, for which a prize had been offered, he panicked and threatened to revert to the behaviours previously recorded, stating it was pointless as his work would be hopeless anyway. When offered a scribe he provided some sound ideas. He didn't win a prize for his workbook but, to his amazement – and his Mum's delight – did get the prize for the person who had shown the most consistent interest and involvement. Whether this will have a knock-on effect on his confidence and behaviour in lessons has yet to be seen.

Tom does not have a diagnosis of dyslexia. However, similar student-centred support would work for him and help to prevent the types of incidents which have resulted in him being termed 'unteachable'.

You will find that you have students in your class like Tom. You may also have those who have dyspraxic type difficulties – so-called 'clumsy child' syndrome – which can affect co-ordination, articulation of words and relations with peers. There will also be those whose difficulties with concentration and/or literacy lead to behaviours sometimes attributed to Attention Deficit Disorder (ADD). There will always be a number of students whose difficulties with speech and language will adversely affect their relationships with peers and teachers, their ability to pick up new subject-specific vocabulary and their oral and written expression. There may also be individuals who fall onto the Autistic spectrum and show the rigid behaviours and difficulties with understanding social conventions and other people's viewpoints typical of Asperger's Syndrome. Mathematics teachers will find that dyslexic students encounter difficulties with the language aspects and sequencing demands of mathematics and that, from time to time, a student exhibits the profound difficulties associated with dyscalculia. These specific difficulties can all co-exist with dyslexia so you should have some awareness of the needs profile associated with each.

Chapters in Part 2 of this book will consider some of these differences, and how they affect behaviour, literacy, numeracy and study skills. You should take the time to consider the pressures your specific curriculum area makes on each of these skills and how you can adapt your teaching to compensate for any weaknesses. The current chapter explores the ways in which the differences linked with SpLD/dyslexia affect general behaviour, both at home and at school.

By the time students come to you, they are likely to have been experiencing failure within primary school and at home for at least eight years so you need to understand the effect this may have had upon their sense of themselves as learners. At home, day-to-day problems tend to be linked with unreliable memory or organisational skills. Inside school, the difficulties associated with the processing of letter or numeric symbols, speed and memory, impinge upon an individual's phonological awareness, ability to read and spell across most languages. They also affect a student's ability to memorise lists, follow instructions, store and maintain verbal information and retrieve phonological information, such as vocabulary, from long-term memory.

How does dyslexia affect home life?

These areas are likely to have caused frustration and conflict at home and it should not be forgotten that the genetic element in SpLD/dyslexia (Stein, 2004) means that parents may themselves have dyslexia and be coping with similar difficulties.

- Memory;
- sequencing;
- concepts of time;
- orientation and left–right confusion;
- automaticity and managing simultaneous activities.

We are all likely to be embarrassed from time to time by 'dyslexic-type' or 'senior' moments when we muddle our words or forget our appointments or equipment because of tiredness, stress or loss of concentration. For the individual with dyslexia, however, this can be normal. A good night's sleep doesn't change anything. Getting through the normal demands of a multi-tasked day will include battling with the written word in the form of TV guides, shopping lists and remembering what you have to do at what time. People with dyslexia often seem to attribute super-human powers of memory to those without dyslexia and feel doubly embarrassed and frustrated when they make mistakes with tasks which they feel, often wrongly, that any fool can do.

So how do memory difficulties make life difficult? There is a mass of research into memory (see Pickering (2004) for details). To oversimplify, memory processing can be seen as a simple moving of information, by way of a range of information-processing strategies, from a short-term processing 'box' into a long-term memory store. Although oversimplified, it is a helpful way of understanding memory processing. People with dyslexia can be described as frequently having difficulties both with the processing and storage of information in the short-term working-memory box and with the retrieval of information from the long-term store. Memory processing, or working memory, includes four major components: the audio memory, the visual memory, movement or procedural memory and the semantic memory (storage of the meanings of words). A weakness in any of these channels puts pressure upon the others.

What types of tasks involve short- or long-term memory? Remembering phone numbers, remembering what you need to take to school, remembering what your sister asked you to buy from the shop. Sequencing also causes difficulty. Combine sequencing with remembering and the problems multiply. Asking an individual to remember several instructions in sequence, when they are not fully attending, or to rely upon spoken instructions only, particularly if the instructions are given under pressure to get things right, is highly likely to result in embarrassing failure. Unfortunately, many everyday tasks do indeed involve sequences of instructions or simultaneous activities. 'While you're taking the rubbish to the bins, please could you put these letters in the car and close the gate?' could end up with letters in the bin, rubbish outside the gate and bad temper all round. If the simplicity of the tasks and the stupidity of the child are then pointed out, the end result will be a reduction in offers of help or co-operation as the child decides he or she would rather be seen as a grumpy teen than an idiot.

Much of practical daily life revolves around sequencing. Alphabetical order and times-tables are an obvious hurdle. However, some learners with dyslexia have little concept of the seasons, months or even days of the week and label their days by the different activities linked with them rather than any concept of Monday to Sunday. Pollock and her colleagues (2004) remind us that there are teenagers who will tell you that summer comes before spring and after autumn. Memory tends to erase all but the most interesting events and activities, removing further points of reference. I remember September because that's my birthday month and November for Guy Fawkes but October contains nothing memorable to me so it gets lost. How can I remember to take my swimming gear to school on Thursday if I haven't noticed that it's Wednesday today because I was more interested in Friday when I will go to football training? To add to the embarrassment, everyone else seems to find this stuff so easy and is quick to point this out. By the time he or she goes to secondary school, an average child usually tells the time competently and is on top of planning the activities, from tennis to shopping days, that make up his or her week. Learners with dyslexia, however, are frequently challenged by the skills needed for telling the time – the spatial and directional skills, the way we talk about numbers, the memory and the sequencing. They can also have little sense of how much time has passed, how long half an hour or three minutes 'feels like' and can struggle with temporal concepts such as 'yesterday', 'today' and 'tomorrow'. Difficulties with automaticity, which chase all other considerations from the mind, when absorbed in an activity, can also lead to minor disasters at home: chores incomplete, dinners burnt, appointments missed. However at school, with its timetables and need for specific equipment at specific times, a seemingly able student can exasperate teachers by his disorganisation, which can be seen as a sign of laziness or lack of commitment.

Orientation and left–right confusion is possibly linked with the late development of handedness in some people with dyslexia, many of whom have problems with visuo-spatial orientation and 'left' and 'right' due, perhaps, to labelling or memory difficulties. As a result some people with dyslexia find it hard to follow a map or plan. These separate day-to-day difficulties are all exacerbated by the cerebellar-based difficulties with automaticity. We are all constantly expected to be able to 'multi-task'. Many of us find this stressful but asking someone with SpLD/dyslexia to attend to more than one thing at a time may be simply asking for trouble.

The impact of SpLD/dyslexia at school

Early Years

For most children with dyslexia, early childhood is unaffected. The child is a happy, lively, pre-schooler, lots of busy fun, fascinated by the world and seems to be the sort of child who should love the early years of school with its dough, construction and play-based activities. Most will get through reception without a glitch – even though they may seem to be bringing home reading books with rather more pictures and fewer words than their parents might expect. Even if her mother expresses concern that Anna seems to be falling behind her best friend in reading, the teacher at this stage will usually say that children all develop at different rates, that Anna is happy, has lots of friends and is taking everything in so they should not worry. This is true for many children but, unfortunately, not for all.

The primary school

The child is now coming up against some things that are difficult for those with dyslexia. Learning to read and write means mastering the sequence of the order of the letters of the alphabet, telling the difference between letter sounds and remembering the ways in which they match the complex letter patterns of English spelling. He or she is probably unable to store the visual images of words in his or her long-term memory and therefore reads by having a stab at the word from the first letter. In some cases the child deceives the teacher for some time by learning the text by heart and making clever guesses. Difficulties with the language of mathematics, with sequencing and remembering numbers, and the different ways in which numbers can face combine into a total mystery. For some children this may be the first time they have encountered failure and disapproval from others in the class, parents or adults. They may well be finding it hard to follow instructions and to remember what teachers have asked them to do.

This may well be the moment when the teacher, puzzled and frustrated, warns the parents that the child is beginning to misbehave, and, unconvinced that the failures of this seemingly able child are caused by anything other than naughtiness, suggests that the child is lazy, careless or difficult. For the parents, this may well be the very first indicator that their child has a learning difficulty and this is already affecting the way that child feels about herself and other children or adults. Behaviour problems can now indeed begin to emerge as children develop avoidance strategies to protect themselves from exposure to failure and ridicule. These can include anything from biting the child at the next desk to playing the class clown. Other children may well be beginning to taunt or avoid them. The teacher may suggest to parents that the child is having difficulty making friends. These children are likely to be distressed by their failures, by the fact that no one seems to realise how hard they try and bewildered by their perception that everyone else seems to be able to do everything so easily and so quickly. They begin to develop a sense of themselves as not being learners – a truly negative learning identity which is reinforced by repeated failure and the way in which teachers label them and their attempts at work.

The secondary school

The difficulties which emerged in the primary school are unlikely to be resolved without informed support and it is hard to underestimate the demoralising effect of repeated failure upon a child as he or she arrives at the secondary school. There are also some children who have coped fairly adequately at primary level but whose skills are vulnerable to the changing demands and context of the secondary school.

On a practical level, imagine the stress of the first day in a large secondary school where the dyslexic student, dependent on maps and timetables he cannot interpret adequately, spends the whole day anxious and lost, trying to find out where his or her group is supposed to be. He is away from the comfort zone – or discomfort zone, depending on the circumstances – of people from his old school who knew him and hoping that his new school might provide him with a new start away from the stigma of failure that he may have experienced at the primary school.

Unless his new school is truly dyslexia-friendly and handles this transition in a sensitive way, any hope may well be misplaced. There will be changes in the way the curriculum is delivered, away from a more experience-based multi-sensory mode of delivery to the more verbal and auditory modes common in the secondary curriculum. There will be a huge number of teachers involved with him in a broad range of locations, new routines and new rules. These challenges also frequently coincide with the beginnings of the mental and physical changes associated with puberty and adolescence and with the child's move from seeking support and approval from family carers to his or her peer group. It is not surprising if, at this stage, when difficulties continue, children opt to impress their peers with challenging behaviour in order to conceal their learning difficulties. It is not cool to be a non-reader.

It is at this stage, with this history, that he or she will come into your classroom. Refresh your understanding of the definitions and causal theories of SpLD/dyslexia. Consider the behaviours you might look for. Would you spot this student? Carry on now to Chapter 3 which will look in more detail at the types of assessment you might be involved in.

A SUMMARY OF **KEY POINTS**

> **The impact of the type of educational failure experienced by students with dyslexia affects them throughout their adult lives.**

> Much of this failure stems from the lack of awareness of the impact that dyslexic type difficulties can have upon a learner's ability to cope with seemingly simple tasks.

> It is essential for teachers to identify the demands made by their subject area and to understand how dyslexia can reduce a student's ability to cope with these, despite interest and knowledge.

> Dyslexic type difficulties will manifest themselves in behaviour, memory and organisational skills, literacy, numeracy and study skills. These come under intense pressure on transfer to secondary school.

MOVING *ON* > > > > > > MOVING *ON* > > > > > > MOVING *ON*

The next stage is to use your growing understanding of how dyslexia may manifest itself in behaviour to consider how your subject might challenge the dyslexic learner.

REFLECTIVE TASK

Identify two of your students who might seem to be showing signs of this pattern of behaviour. What might you consider doing next?

Select one suggestion from the chapter and review and reflect on its implications for your teaching.

FURTHER READING FURTHER READING **FURTHER READING** FURTHER READING

Mortimore, T (2008) *Dyslexia and learning style. A practical handbook.* 2nd edition. Chichester: Wiley.

Ott, P (2007) *Teaching children with dyslexia. A practical guide*. Abingdon: Routledge.

Pollock, J, Waller, E and Politt, R (2004) *Day-to-day dyslexia in the classroom.* 2nd Edition. Abingdon: Routledge Falmer.

Reid, G (2005) *Dyslexia*. London: Continuum.

3
How might you 'measure' dyslexia?

Chapter objectives

By the end of this chapter you should:

- **be able to make links between the definitions of dyslexia, the behaviours you see in the classroom and how we 'measure' these to identify a person as dyslexic;**
- **understand the difference between a screening test and an assessment;**
- **be able to make links between measurements of dyslexia and how these are used to develop successful support strategies in the classroom;**
- **understand your role in providing support as part of that provision and in monitoring student progress;**
- **have laid the foundations for understanding your role as part of the team, as discussed further in Chapter 9.**

This chapter addresses the following Professional Standards for QTS and Core:

Q12, Q26, C12, C14

Introduction

Chapters 1 and 2 defined dyslexia and looked at some of the behaviours that you may observe in your classroom that are linked to dyslexia. You have already read that as many as 10% of the students in your classroom may have dyslexia and so it is tempting to think that, by the time a student arrives at secondary school, his or her dyslexia will have been identified and a successful intervention programme put in place to meet any needs. In addition there will have been liaison between the feeder primary school and secondary school to ensure a happy and positive transition. In some instances this policy becomes best practice, but the case studies in Chapter 2 demonstrated that this was not always the reality. So, as a newly qualified teacher entering a classroom for the first time, what is your role in measuring dyslexia and in supporting intervention programmes?

Picture this. It is your first parents' evening and two anxious parents arrive at your desk to discuss their child's first term at secondary school. They listen intently as you talk about their child and discuss his behaviour in class, his homework and his grades for work. They look anxious and depressed. Then they say, 'You do *know* that Gregory has dyslexia, don't you?' You look anxious because you did not know. You are the third teacher they have listened to, all have described similar traits and they all link to Gregory's dyslexia. No one seems to know Gregory has dyslexia. There is a difference between identifying dyslexia and having it formally assessed. Not all students in your classroom will have had a formal assessment for dyslexia by the time they reach you.

PRACTICAL TASK PRACTICAL TASK **PRACTICAL TASK** PRACTICAL TASK **PRACTICAL TASK**

Having read Chapters 1 and 2 make a list of the opportunities there may have been to identify a student's dyslexia before the start of secondary school.

PRACTICAL TASK PRACTICAL TASK PRACTICAL TASK PRACTICAL TASK PRACTICAL TASK

Here are some of the common ways of identifying dsylexia before entering secondary school:

- observation by nursery school teachers;
- classroom observation by teachers and support workers;
- poor results at Key Stage 1 Literacy national tests;
- parental concern at lack of progress and/or comparison to siblings' progress;
- early good start to developing literacy skills progress halted;
- discrepancy between maths, science and English national tests results at Key Stage 2;
- assessment by SENCo;
- assessment by LA Specialist support team;
- private assessment by dyslexia specialist teacher or educational psychologist paid for by parents.

Making links between the definitions and the 'measurement' of dyslexia

You will remember from Chapter 1 that there is increasing neurological evidence of brain differences in people with dyslexia. Those who support the controversial medical model of dyslexia might suggest that every child could have a PET brain scan at pre school level, with perhaps a blood test to identify genetic differences, and hence their dyslexia could be identified and provision made. Currently the identification of dyslexia is the province of the educational profession – unlike SpLDs, such as autistic spectrum disorder, Attention Deficit (Hyperactivity) Disorder (AD(H)D) and dyspraxia, which are identified and managed by multi disciplinary teams including GPs, speech therapists, and occupational therapists, as well as educationalists. Like every educational resource there are always political, financial and pedagogical influences that affect the epidemiological identification of dyslexia.

In this section you will reflect on the assessment process for dyslexia and how students have access to this process in line with the 'graduated approach through School Action and School Action Plus' (Code of Practice 2001) for all students with SEN (Special Educational Needs). This process means that children whose progress or profile gives cause for concern start off by being placed on 'School Action' which means that they are usually provided with an IEP (Individual Education Plan) and their individual progress is monitored before, if necessary, moving on to the more detailed and specific School Action Plus level which precedes the compilation of a Statement of Special Educational Needs if School Action Plus does not provide adequate support. Do not worry – as a newly qualified teacher you are not expected to take on this specialist assessment or role – but an understanding of the terminology and assessment process will help you fulfil your class teacher role of providing a dyslexia-friendly classroom as part of this assessment and in understanding and delivering elements of a student's IEP or GEP (Group Education Plan).

PRACTICAL TASK PRACTICAL TASK PRACTICAL TASK PRACTICAL TASK PRACTICAL TASK

Look at the Dyslexia Action definition of dyslexia again. Highlight the words that would guide you to what needs to be 'measured' in order to suggest a person has dyslexia.

Dyslexia is a specific learning difficulty that mainly affects reading and spelling. Dyslexia is characterised by difficulties in processing word-sounds and by weaknesses in short-term verbal memory; its effects may be seen in spoken language as well as written language. The current evidence suggests that these difficulties arise from inefficiencies in language-processing areas in the left hemisphere of the brain which, in turn, appear to be linked to genetic differences.

Dyslexia is life-long, but its effects can be minimised by targeted literacy intervention, technological support and adaptations to ways of working and learning. Dyslexia is not related to intelligence, race or social background. Dyslexia varies in severity and often occurs alongside other specific learning diffi-culties, such as Dyspraxia or Attention Deficit Disorder, resulting in variation in the degree and nature of individuals' strengths and weaknesses.

Dyslexia Action (Formerly Dyslexia Institute) 21.10.07

You should have found the following:

- reading;
- spelling;
- processing word-sounds;
- short-term verbal memory;
- spoken language;
- written language.

You may have also added

Intelligence. (Remember that Chapter 2 cautioned against linking dyslexia and intelligence. However, it can be a useful *additional* piece of evidence in a student's learning profile.)

A full assessment for dyslexia

So in order to assess and label someone as 'dyslexic' or 'having dyslexia' we would need to measure all of the above **and** have evidence that the person's scores were lower than expected for students of a similar age and educational experience in the areas above. Some of these measurements are for attainment, such as reading and spelling. Other measurements are for underlying abilities, such as processing sounds and short term verbal memory.

Such assessments are the province of educational psychologists and teachers who have a specialist post graduate diploma in the theory, assessment and teaching of children and adults with dyslexia. Many assessment tools are 'closed tools' for use only by those specia-lists who are qualified to use and most importantly **interpret** assessment scores. The tools used to measure these differences are constantly refined and developed using large popula-tion groups of children or adults to find the 'usual' from which to distinguish and measure the 'unusual'. Score tables are always related to specific age groups and so an accurate assessment will have used the correct up to date assessment tools, with the correct ceiling ages for the tests and person being assessed. For example, the Neale Analysis of Reading Ability is a useful assessment tool for measuring reading accuracy and comprehension. However, its ceiling use is for children aged 12 and below, so it is not of much use to measure reading development and access to text books in someone in year 10 about to embark on a GCSE course.

Most assessment tools used to assess for dyslexia are objective. That is, they use standardised measurements and scores. Test scores are given in a variety of ways. Most non professionals prefer to see an age equivalent score which measures a child's score against their age. For example a child of 12 years 2 months old, scoring a reading age of 12 years 1 month would be said to be performing within expected limits. Age equivalent scores are less useful as a child becomes older as they tend to 'flatten out'. Professionals use percentile ranks and standardised scores. Percentile ranks range from 1 to 100. This means that a child scoring a percentile rank of 50 is average, of 10 is below average and of 80 is above average. Standardised scores are also used which range from 40 to 160; in this instance a score of 100 would be average. The Warnock Report (1978) noted that at any one time roughly 2% of the school population would have a need severe enough to warrant a Statement of Special Educational Need. Whilst Mary Warnock regrets the way this phrase was used literally, it is a reflection of the way such standardised scores and percentile ranks have been used. Often, a student would need to be on the 2nd percentile or lower, performing less well than 98% of his or her peers in areas of difficulty associated with dyslexia, in order to be eligible for a statement.

An assessment for a diagnosis of dyslexia will measure an individual's profile of learning strengths and weaknesses: reading skills, both reading accuracy and reading comprehension, spelling skills, intellectual ability and the underlying cognitive weaknesses associated with dyslexia – most importantly the phonological skills differences and memory difficulties that were discussed in Chapter 1. It will also look at learning strengths and subjective assessments, such as writing ability and organisational skills. These will be seen in the context of a student's educational background and medical history. (A student who has attended five primary schools in four years, or who has been absent due to severe ear infections may display similar achievements and abilities in some areas to someone with a specific learning difficulty.) The diagnosis and severity of dyslexia will then be noted in a concluding paragraph within an assessment.

It is unlikely that as a classroom teacher you will be asked to read an assessment for dyslexia, either by a parent or by your SENCo. If you are, a careful read of the conclusion will alert you to whether the dyslexia is mild, moderate or severe. A further section will offer suggestions for support and intervention and it is this section you should read carefully. We will return to this later in the chapter.

So which of the students in your class are likely to have had a full assessment for dyslexia? All of the students in your class who have a Statement of Special Educational Need for dyslexia will have had a full assessment, usually by an educational psychologist but sometimes by an area specialist support teacher. Some LAs are still reluctant to use the term 'dyslexia' preferring still to refer to 'severe difficulties with the acquisition of literacy skills', or a 'specific learning difficulty'.

Students in your class who are placed on the Code of Practice at School Action Plus may have had a full assessment and diagnosis through the LA for their dyslexia. In addition, you may have a student in your class, on School Action, whose parents have paid privately for an assessment of dyslexia. Their level of difficulty is such that they are unlikely ever to be assessed by the specialist advisory team or LA educational psychologist. As was noted in Chapter 2, self-esteem can be damaged by a student's repeated failure or lack of recognition for their dyslexia. Parents who can afford it may pay for a private assessment. Such assessments will note a diagnosis where there is evidence to suggest it. They cannot place the student on a stage of the Code of Practice, this is the role of the SENCo. However, their reports should be taken just as seriously by you. Most students assessed privately are less likely to have severe difficulties, and will be placed on the Code of Practice School Action. In these instances you may be the only intermediary in creating a dyslexia-friendly classroom and supporting them to access the curriculum. As the classroom teacher you can make a huge difference in the educational journey of such students. (Adults with dyslexia when questioned about their school experiences state they wanted understanding and patience far more than expertise.)

If we return to Gregory at parents' evening you now have some questions you could ask, and actions you could take.

● Who assessed Gregory?
● When was Gregory assessed?
● What level of severity is Gregory's dyslexia?
● Does the SENCo have Gregory's assessment?

If Gregory was assessed and the school SENCo knows and has not told you, or he was placed by his primary school on the graduated approach to special needs through School Action or School Action Plus and the SENCo has not told you, all you can do is apologise and promise to follow up later. As a newly qualified teacher, make coded notes on your class registers of all students placed on the Code and if possible the reason for their placement, e.g. SAPdys (School Action Plus, dyslexia). This will give you a gentle reminder of your responsibility, every lesson as you take your register.

You do not have to be an expert or experienced teacher to realise that very few of the estimated 10% of students in your class who exhibit signs of dyslexia will have had a full assessment and an 'official diagnosis' of dyslexia.

PRACTICAL TASK PRACTICAL TASK **PRACTICAL TASK** PRACTICAL TASK **PRACTICAL TASK**

Think about the access to formal diagnoses of dyslexia. Make a list of the pros and cons of being formally identified as having dyslexia.

For those who never receive a formal diagnosis of dyslexia there are other ways of measuring dyslexia that are available to schools. These can be used to note students' patterns of strengths and weaknesses in order to provide them with support throughout school and to act as guidance in correct placement on the Code of Practice for SEN.

Screening tools and processes

A screening process is an attempt to identify individuals within a group who are likely to present with a specific set of patterns you are looking for. It can be used to identify likely 'at risk' groups or individuals. Screening processes for identifying possible students at risk of having dyslexia are no different. They will look at a profile of strengths and weaknesses and use these to predict the likelihood that a student has dyslexia. As screening tools they are not as accurate as full assessments, and should not be used to give a diagnosis. Screening processes can vary. You may have been subject to such a screening process yourself as you entered HE or your PGCE course, without being aware.

There are several commercial screening tools, some computerised, such as the LASS Secondary (Lucid Assessment Systems for Schools, Secondary Edition. Beverley, East Yorkshire: Lucid Creative Ltd. 1999) and paper based tools such as the DST (Dyslexia Screening Test (Nicholson and Fawcett: 1996). These are available for use with individuals from preschool age into adulthood. Computerised screening tools have the advantage that they can deliver and interpret the scores obtained and use them to predict the outcome. (It was noted earlier that an assessment tool is only as good as the interpreter of that tool.) They are also quicker and cheaper to administer than an assessment. They can give a school an indication of the resource needs in relation to a group or year of students and help to monitor progress. Screening tools have some disadvantages; they can give what are known as 'false positives' i.e. identify a student at risk when there is no dyslexia, and 'false negatives' i.e. fail to identify a student at risk. If you search the internet for screening tools and dyslexia you will see a wealth of choice. Commercialised screening tools for dyslexia are often used within primary schools, as part of a school's SEN identification policy and you may have students in your class whose profile of strengths and weaknesses has been identified using screening tools and their support programme and place on the Code of Practice for SEN based on such evidence.

By now you will have gathered that this graduated approach through school action and school action plus is linked to how you might measure dyslexia. So far we have thought about the students identified using formal assessment measurements. But if you cast your thoughts back to the list of assessment opportunities that you collected for activity one, you can see that there are several ways in which dyslexia can be measured by class teachers. The purpose of any test or assessment must not only be to measure but to do something with the outcome. Teachers are constantly assessing individuals. Lack of progress in national test scores as a pupil progresses from Key Stage 1 through to Key Stage 3 are a useful way of measuring the possibility of the presence of dyslexia. This is particularly so with those students whose difficulties are less severe. A well motivated student with good peer support may have been able to mask difficulties in the primary school. Parents may have been working hard at the school gate talking to other parents and daily to the class teacher to ensure a high level of support both in school and at home. These students may enter secondary school having just reached an overall level 4 in their English national test. This may mask a student who gained a good level 4 in reading and a weak level 3 in writing. They may have learning strengths in science and maths. A student with such a profile would not be on the school's special needs register, and would not have been highlighted to the SENCo as part of the school's transition and liaison policy. As the pressures and demands of the secondary school curriculum increase, and the link between home and school becomes dependent on the home–school diary, such students may begin to fall behind. So you may well be in the position of starting to realise the possibility of identifying a student with dyslexia in your own classroom.

Consider these two case studies and how they fit into the story of how we measure dyslexia.

CASE STUDY 1

Jodie entered nursery school unable to talk. By the time she was in Year 1 she was talking at a level appropriate for her age but struggling with early reading skills. She was an 'August birthday', so everyone agreed not to worry and that she would 'catch up' soon. At the beginning of Year 2 Jodie was placed on School Action, and given an IEP. Her IEP concentrated on additional support for her reading, the teaching of high frequency words and phonic skills and teaching assistant support, as Jodie found it difficult to concentrate. In Year 3 Jodie's mum expressed concern at parents' evening over Jodie's lack of concentration, difficult behaviour at home and refusal to read her reading book to her parents each evening. She had visited the GP who suggested Jodie might have hyperactivity. Jodie's literacy skills development was still behind that of her classmates and she found it difficult to listen during class based activities. At the end of Year 3 Jodie scored level 2c in her optional English national test, but did well in her optional mathematics national test which was read to her. Her class teacher noted that Jodie was popular in class, able to express herself well and had been voted onto the school council by her peers. The SENCo moved Jodie to School Action Plus and sought the advice of the LA's advisory teacher. After observing Jodie in class, talking to Jodie's class teacher and conducting additional achievement and ability tests, the advisory teacher suggested Jodie might have dyslexic type difficulties. She wrote an intervention programme, which focussed on phonological skills development and Jodie's support hours were increased. Jodie took part in wave 3 intervention programmes.

By Year 5 Jodie's progress was significantly behind her peers'. Her Optional English national test scores still showed her functioning at level 2c, and the advisory teacher assessed that her standardised scores for reading and spelling had fallen from the 5 percentile rank to 3. At the beginning of Year 6, Jodie's class teacher, SENCo and advisory teacher, in consultation with Jodie's parents, suggested she should be considered for a Statement of Special Educational Need. Jodie received her statement in the spring term before her transition to secondary school. The Educational Psychologist confirmed the diagnosis of dyslexia, and in addition she was diagnosed with comorbid difficulties of ADHD. Before transition to her secondary school, the primary school SENCo met with the SENCo of the secondary school. Jodie was placed in a tutorial group with her best friend for support, and in small groups for English and mathematics. The secondary school SENCo ensured all subject heads and class teachers were aware of Jodie's difficulties using a pen portrait (a short description of Jodie's learning strengths and weaknesses, together with her IEP targets). She received teaching assistant support in all areas of the curriculum where there is a heavy dependency on literacy skills.

Jodie's profile is typical of those of many students who have a Statement of SEN for dyslexia. The process involved intervention and monitoring over several years with a team of learning support assistants, class teachers, the SENCo and the specialist advisory teacher. It demonstrates that Jodie's dyslexia was 'measured' in different ways over time.

CASE STUDY 2

Mark is in Year 9. His brother is in Year 11 and has a statement of SEN for dyslexia. Mark is hard working and was identified as being at risk of dyslexia during his early years at primary school, where the SEN policy was to screen all children on entry. The primary school used a whole school structured phonics programme for all children and Mark's progress was monitored by the class teacher. He made good progress during primary school and was never placed on the school's special needs register. Mark entered his secondary school with average national test scores in English (level 4) and above average national test scores in science and mathematics (level 5). Mark is hard working, but recently has fallen behind with his homework. His end of school report notes that his exam results at the end of each year are disappointing and do not reflect his ability in class. As his form tutor and current English teacher you have noticed his lack of organisational skills and having just started to study the Shakespeare text were surprised when Mark could not read aloud accurately. You ask Mark after the lesson if he is finding Year 9 difficult. He says that he is. You ask him if he would mind you discussing your concerns with the SENCo. The SENCo uses the LASS screening assessment tool. This highlights that Mark is struggling with his literacy skills and that the underlying problems with phonological skills and memory skills still persist. The LASS assessment suggests that Mark will be eligible for special exam arrangements. The SENCo discusses the results with Mark and his form teacher. She talks to Mark's parents and suggests that Mark would benefit from being given extra time for all end of unit tests in school and for the end of Year 9 national tests. She suggests that Mark attend five sessions with her to discuss adaptations to his ways of working and learning, using technology aids and organisation skills tools. At the weekly staff meeting the SENCo highlights Mark as having been identified as in need of additional support and she adds him to the group education plan (GEP) for students with mild to moderate difficulties. On the GEP she notes Mark's learning strengths and weaknesses. All staff are aware of barriers to learning in their subject areas for students who have memory difficulties and phonological difficulties and make adaptations to support such students.

Mark is placed on the school's SEN Code of Practice at School Action. His needs are met by his class teachers. Early intervention by his English teacher, quick accessible screening tools from the SENCo, and secure whole school strategies ensure that Mark is back on track for success. Mark's story is typical of students with mild dyslexia. Their needs change over time. Should Mark progress to Higher Education, he is likely to be eligible for support and the Disabled Student's Allowance (DSA). For such allowances he will eventually require a full assessment from an eligible assessor. For now, this is not necessary.

Case study 2 illustrates how classroom teachers provide support for students with dyslexia, and that this support can be at the personalised level with the aid of whole school strategies that remove barriers to learning. The two case studies have introduced you to the range of practitioners that will form part of the team in identifying, supporting and monitoring the effectiveness of the support for students with dyslexia.

At each stage of this 'measurement' a profile of a student's strengths as well as their weaknesses is identified. This can then aid in the provision of a personalised programme of intervention. As a teacher new to the classroom, always remember to focus on what your students can do, as well as what they cannot do, when your opinion is sought.

Conclusion

Dyslexia is a specific learning difficulty for which there are useful, reliable assessment tools. These assessment tools can be used to establish a profile of learning strengths and weaknesses from which a successful intervention programme can be written. Not all students within your classroom will have had a formal assessment to identify their dyslexia. By creating a dyslexia-friendly classroom, as discussed in Chapter 4, you will create a safe, personalised learning environment for all students with dyslexia, whether this has been identified or not.

A SUMMARY OF **KEY POINTS**

> **There is a range of approaches to assessment which includes formative and summative assessment.**

> **Assessment forms part of the graduated response to need within the Code of Practice (2001) and should be linked to provision.**

> **Many dyslexic learners in your classroom will not have been identified nor had a formal assessment.**

MOVING *ON* > > > **>** **>** **>** MOVING *ON* > > > **>** **>** **>** MOVING *ON*

Make a list of all the students whom you teach, who have been placed on the Code of Practice for SpLD/ dyslexia.

Make a list of any students in your class that you suspect may have dyslexia but are not on the list above. What behaviours have you seen that lead you to suspect they may have dyslexia?

Make sure you are familiar with, and use, all the whole school policies in place to prevent barriers to learning in your school.

FURTHER READING FURTHER READING **FURTHER READING** FURTHER READING

Backhouse, G and Morris, K (2005) *Dyslexia: Assessing and reporting. The patoss guide.* London: Patoss.

DfES *Code of Practice* (2001).

For a more in-depth exploration of assessment and SpLD, see Turner, M (1997) *Psychological assessment of dyslexia*. London: Whurr Publishers.

4
The dyslexia-friendly classroom

Chapter objectives

By the end of this chapter you should:

- **have been reminded of the concept of 'inclusion' discussed in the Introduction, and considered how you can adapt your classroom and your teaching to ensure that dyslexic learners will be included. Remember:**

  It is clear from research and practice that what is educationally sound for dyslexic learners is of value to all, particularly when learning in a mainstream inclusive classroom. (Peer, 2004, p157)

- **have an overview of the types of adjustments that can be made to create the dyslexia-friendly classroom. Specific strategies and ideas for specific areas of the curriculum will be developed in Chapters 6 and 7. You should currently be focussing upon the types of differences that might apply to all aspects of the curriculum.**

This chapter addresses the following Professional Standards for QTS and Core:

Q3b, Q10, Q12, Q20, Q26a, Q30, Q31, C21, C33, C34, C35, C36, C37, C38, C39

Introduction

The first part of this book introduced you to the learning differences that accompany dyslexia and to some ways of identifying those students who might be experiencing this type of difficulty. However, since a minimum of 4% of the learners you encounter may well be diagnosed with dyslexia at some stage in their lives (Singleton, 1999), it is highly likely, as suggested in Chapter 3, that you will teach students whose dyslexia has not yet been identified. You will need to be prepared to take immediate action to ensure that your teaching will empower these students rather than waiting for assessments or diagnoses. The British Dyslexia Association (2006) emphasises that many of the difficulties in acquiring skills experienced by dyslexic learners are exacerbated by the policies and practices established in educational institutions. It is therefore up to all teachers to be alert to the need to avoid creating barriers through their choice of teaching methods or classroom management.

We have already explored the strengths and weaknesses that accompany dyslexia and the impact that they can have upon behaviour and self-esteem if needs are not met. How best can you support these people in your classroom and help them to gain real satisfaction from their learning?

How might inclusion in a mainstream classroom affect dyslexic learners?

You might like to discuss all these activities with a colleague or mentor.

PRACTICAL TASK PRACTICAL TASK **PRACTICAL TASK** PRACTICAL TASK **PRACTICAL TASK**

What types of differences might dyslexic learners display?

Look back at Part 1 of this book and collect together, on the second chart, the strengths and weaknesses a dyslexic learner might show. Consider the impact of these difficulties upon learning and which might be the most restrictive. The first chart provides some examples to help you.

Chart One

Strengths	Weaknesses	Impact upon classroom experience
e.g. Good reasoning skills		e.g. Able to participate fully in content of sessions. Ability may be underestimated if judged from written work. Frustrated and embarrassed by difficulties with literacy.
	Poor reading skills	e.g. Inability to read worksheets or from board. Inability to keep up with the reading activities in the classroom.
e.g. Good reasoning skills		e.g. Able to participate fully in content of sessions. Ability may be underestimated if judged from written work. Frustrated and embarrassed by difficulties with literacy.
	Poor reading skills	e.g. Inability to read worksheets or from board. Inability to keep up with the reading activities in the classroom.
e.g. Good reasoning skills		e.g. Able to participate fully in content of sessions. Ability may be underestimated if judged from written work. Frustrated and embarrassed by difficulties with literacy.
	Poor reading skills	e.g. Inability to read worksheets or from board. Inability to keep up with the reading activities in the classroom.

Chart Two

Strengths	Weaknesses	Impact upon classroom experience

This will give you a picture of the types of difficulties which arise from dyslexic differences and the ways in which classroom environments and teaching might need to be adjusted to remove barriers.

Do all dyslexic learners experience the same difficulties?

You will be aware that all dyslexic learners are individuals with specific patterns of strengths and weaknesses.

PRACTICAL TASK PRACTICAL TASK PRACTICAL TASK PRACTICAL TASK PRACTICAL TASK

(Evidence for Standard 3.2.4)

Look back at the two case study profiles presented in Chapter 3, Jodie and Mark. Fill in the charts to reflect their individual profiles.

Jodie

Strengths	Weaknesses	Impact

Mark

Strengths	Weaknesses	Impact

Consider the barriers to learning they might encounter in your subject classroom.

Jodie	Mark

How might you use their strengths?

Jodie	Mark

This should be typical of the way in which you could consider the needs of those individuals within your groups who may not seem to be flourishing. If your management skills can create a classroom environment which meets the needs of the most vulnerable and frequently the most challenging of your students, you should find that it becomes a more congenial place for everyone.

Creating an inclusive classroom. How can your classroom become dyslexia-friendly?

You will find a clear picture of the inclusive culture which nurtures the dyslexia-friendly classroom in Booth and Ainscow's (2002) *Index for Inclusion*. To summarise, your classroom needs to be a community where everyone feels welcome, where collaboration rather than competition is the norm and where differences are celebrated rather than being the source of tension and criticism. Your attitude, and that of your colleagues, is central to achieving this and will encourage your students to support and respect each other. You will need to ensure that all the 'ingredients' are in place to make this easy. These two ingredients will need to be reviewed, bearing the pattern of dyslexic differences in mind:

- people;
- teaching approaches and their impact upon the way you manage your classroom resources and environment.

People

Team work is crucial to a dyslexia-friendly classroom. *Teachers* are likely to collaborate with *teaching assistants (TAs)*, to value the expertise of the *SENCo*, and to help the *dyslexic students' peers* to understand and support them in many ways. *Parents* are also heavily involved in their children's learning. Chapter 9 will explore how all these people can work as a team across the school – they all have their part to play in establishing the dyslexia-friendly classroom.

Teachers

Exploration of the opinions of dyslexic students (Johnson, 2004) and conversations with experienced specialist teachers suggest that there are some *ground rules for teachers*. You may want to discuss the following with your mentor and colleagues.

Ground rules
- Encourage students' strengths.
- Do not expose their weaknesses.
- Provide opportunities for success (however small) and then praise it. However, beware of hollow praise – your students will see straight through this.
- Ensure that they are aware of the progress they are making.
- Encourage all students to think and talk about the ways in which they learn and then allow them to use their preferences and strengths whenever possible.
- Encourage them also to explain their difficulties to the teacher, TA or supportive peer/s so that you can co-operate to find the best ways to support them to develop independent strategies.
- Try to establish a fairly steady routine to create security and ensure that all students have taken in any instructions you may have given.
- Be prepared to explain many times in many ways but do not publicise a learner's failure to understand.

- Don't expect a dyslexic learner to be able to do two things at once (e.g. write and absorb instructions simultaneously).
- **Never** forget how embarrassing failure is.

The dyslexic learners in Johnson's (2004) study hated teachers who shouted, who rushed them or got stressed when they got things wrong or needed things to be explained. In short, Johnson states:

> *They want calmness and security, the feeling that teachers might actually like them and are enthusiastic about their subject, quiet recognition of their difference and the provision of low-key differentiation and support.*

(p13)

PRACTICAL TASK PRACTICAL TASK **PRACTICAL TASK** PRACTICAL TASK **PRACTICAL TASK**

Select a student you know and go through the list of ground rules, considering how you could put them into action with this particular learner. Focus on a couple of practical activities based on the rules and try them out the next time you meet. Record the outcome and reflect upon the effect this had upon your relationship.

Rule	Activity	Impact

Teaching assistants

Teaching assistants (TAs) play a key part in the process of differentiation and support within the classroom, and well-trained, sensitive TAs are worth their weight in gold. The relationships they can build with students and with you and the insights they bring from seeing your students in other classrooms are invaluable. Chapter 9 will suggest how you can help your TA to become an essential part of your support system.

The SENCo

Chapter 9 also explores the role of the SENCo who will be an invaluable source of expertise and advice in the development of your dyslexia-friendly environment. Make sure that you have talked to him or her before you start to teach and that you are aware of any students within your groups who have any type of special need and what the existing provision is for them. You should be provided with copies of their Individual Educational Plans.

Parents and links with home

An inclusive culture highlights the partnership between school and parents/carers and you are likely to be the first, and therefore vital, link in this chain. The majority of parents are deeply involved in their children's education and, if a child has been struggling, may well be concerned, be keen to help and work with you and feel frustrated by any seeming lack of progress. There may well be 'history' where the parent feels, rightly or wrongly, that schools have let them down, so you may have bridges to build. Chapter 9 will provide you with further help for welcoming parents into the team, however, this team building work is likely to start with you as you have both the opportunity and the practical reasons to be in contact with them.

Two practical areas which will bring you into contact with parents will be organisation and homework. There is huge potential for grief in both of these, but if you communicate and work together they can also build helpful bridges. Tips for helping co-operation and encouraging good organisation and to make homework into a constructive activity are offered in Chapters 8 and 9.

Homework

The worth of homework remains contentious; however, teachers are often under pressure to set it. Parents have been known to complain if their children do not get set homework and then to complain that it is a source of conflict and difficult to complete. You will need to be clear what your school policy is regarding homework and what your personal position is. You will also need to be clear as to whether you are going to set the same homework for all or to differentiate. This can be, of course, a minefield. Whatever you decide, always be sure that the homework is useful. The following ground rules apply:

- be sure the homework is necessary;
- be sure the dyslexic learner has it written down correctly, knows what to do and when the deadline is;
- be sure that you have estimated correctly how long it might take the majority of the students – and then add at least 25–50% extra time for your dyslexic learners;
- be aware of what other homework is set for that night for other subjects;
- be aware when you have set the dyslexic learner an impossible task e.g. learn 20 spellings; learn the seven times table; write 400 words by tomorrow.

Your relationship with the parents will be crucial for the success of homework and ill-conceived homework will damage it. The parent needs to understand that any homework is necessary. The parent also needs to be able to let you know that her son took forty minutes to write half a side; that he spent an hour with his daughter trying to learn the spellings she subsequently got wrong.

Ground rules for working with parents

- Be aware of the way that their child's difficulties may have upset the family and that you will have to tread carefully.
- Establish a supportive relationship with the parents.
- Set up a clear way of communicating.
- Help the parents to organise the student.

Peers

In secondary school, peers have the power to make or break vulnerable learners. The following story shows how the positive role of peers can be misunderstood and mishandled.

CASE STUDY

John had recently taken over a Year 7 class for science. The class were mostly well motivated, particularly enjoying the experiments, and co-operative when requested to work quietly to write up their work. However, a group of three girls persisted in chattering during this quiet working time whenever John was out of range, despite his reprimanding them loudly and increasingly abruptly from across the classroom. Eventually he forced Sami, Leanne and Susie to sit at separate tables with other groups. Sami and Leanne grumbled but got down to their work. Susie failed to start and when criticised, tore up her work. John sent her out of the classroom. When he demanded an apology, Susie refused rudely. John set her a detention and referred her to her Year Head.

What would you suggest that John should do?

Real life outcome

Reference to the Year Head was the key to this scenario. John had not been informed that Susie, although articulate and interested in science, had difficulties with literacy. Sami, Leanne and Susie had been friends throughout primary school and the three of them co-operated, with Sami and Leanne supporting Susie's reading and spelling and Susie often providing insights into the science. By imposing silent working, John had unwittingly destroyed Susie's support system and the fact that he had abruptly and publicly repri-manded them across the classroom meant that they had been unwilling to share this with him for fear that they were in some way 'cheating'. Susie's subsequent behaviour was impulsive and destructive but it was the only way that she could think of to conceal her difficulty from a new teacher who had indicated that he would be less than sympathetic.

CASE STUDY

Maria was working with a middle ability Year 11 English group. The class were studying *Of Mice and Men* as an exam text and Maria had asked them to take it in turns to read around the class. When she came to Richard, he hesitated and, unheard by Maria, the boy next to him grunted 'Come on, Lennie'. Richard instantly turned and lashed out at him clumsily, missing him and causing complete disruption. Maria punished Richard.

What would you suggest that she should have done differently?

REFLECTIVE TASK

When you have finished this chapter, revisit this section and decide which of the rules of the dyslexia-friendly classroom these two inexperienced teachers have broken and how both situations could have been handled differently to prevent the breakdown and to help to develop inclusive attitudes in the classroom.

Raising awareness in an inclusive community

A crucial responsibility of the inclusive teacher is to attempt to develop an atmosphere where pupils accept diversity of all types and support is offered to anyone at the time when a need emerges. Research has shown that an increase in levels of understanding has been one of the positive outcomes of inclusion. No one pretends that this is easy. Prejudice abounds and pupils who are vulnerable in one way are quick to bully those who are vulnerable in other ways. Children with dyslexia will have been called 'thick', may have been laughed at, humiliated and bullied in class (Scott, 2004). The whole class will need to be made aware of dyslexic role models, both famous people and local older learners. Your role will be to raise awareness, promote understanding, to enable children to show their strengths and to organise students in such a way that the vulnerable are both protected and given the opportunity to develop independent survival strategies. There are a number of ways in which to do this and, as before, there are ground rules which should not be broken.

- Be careful in your use of group work. Group dyslexic children with those who will both support them in their areas of weakness and benefit from their strengths.
- Encourage dyslexic learners to have a 'study buddy'. However be sensitive in your management of this.
- Make all pupils aware of dyslexia and other specific learning differences and that these are not linked with intellectual difficulties. Help them to understand that dyslexia goes beyond problems with literacy and that students with dyslexia may have to concentrate far harder than others to keep themselves organised.
- Never expose a dyslexic learner's weaknesses to his or her peers.

Teaching strategies

A range of subject specific strategies are explored in Part 2 of this book. Here are two principles for helping dyslexic students to learn across the curriculum. The aim is to help you to avoid those approaches which will make life difficult for everyone.

The first principle must be: *teach to strengths*

Dyslexic learners frequently find it hard to process verbal information quickly. Even if they are orally proficient, they will have difficulty expressing their thoughts on paper. You will need to consider the style in which they prefer to learn as research suggests that vulnerable students learn more effectively when the mode of presentation suits their preferred style (Riding and Rayner, 1998). Some may find processing and presenting information visually less threatening. Others may be articulate but need extra time to process information and to marshal their thoughts. You will need to consider ways in which you can help them to discover their strongest channels for different tasks, to think objectively about the ways in which they prefer to learn and you will then need to offer a range of opportunities to enable them to try out different strategies.

This will mean that you need to develop a repertoire of ways of presenting information in a multi-modal way which includes visual, oral, aural and practical methods. You will also need to help your students develop different types of strategies for storing incoming information and for planning written and other presentations which suit their preferences. Reid (2005a), Price (2007) and Mortimore (2008) provide a range of suggestions as to how you can do this, and further strategies will be discussed in Chapter 6. Multi-sensory teaching is recommended as the most effective way of developing literacy in learners with dyslexia. These multi-modal teaching strategies will also appeal to other members of your class who will have their own preferences and will benefit from developing a more metacognitive awareness of their learning processes.

> **PRACTICAL TASK** PRACTICAL TASK PRACTICAL TASK PRACTICAL TASK PRACTICAL TASK
>
> Select a lesson topic that you plan to teach your group. Consider how you might achieve your learning aims using a range of multi-modal methods.

Topic:			
Methods	Visual	Auditory/verbal	Practical

The second principle must be: *avoid overloading the weaker areas*

What are the weaker areas? Which ones are likely to persist throughout secondary education?

1. Planning written work and getting thoughts down on paper.
2. Reading slowly, even when reading seems compensated.
3. Completing tasks at speed.
4. Remembering tasks, learned facts, arrangements, especially if under pressure or overloaded.
5. Copying any material from a black/white board.
6. Absorbing vital lesson instructions.

Weak area 1: written work

Dyslexic students at university continue to experience difficulties with written work and spelling (Riddick et al., 1997; Mortimore, 2006). They also report continuous pressure throughout secondary school (Mortimore and Crozier, 2006). Just as with homework, consider *why* you are asking a dyslexic learner to produce a piece of written work and be very clear as to your purpose. If it is to prepare for a completed piece of course work, make the distinction between the 'ideas' draft where the only criteria should be presenting the ideas and the 'final' draft where spelling, grammar and punctuation become important. Only expect an 'immaculate' piece if it is going on the wall or in the course work folder, and provide support with proofreading.

The purpose of a piece of work should also affect your marking policies and attitudes to mistakes in spelling, grammar, punctuation and handwriting. If a student enthusiastically writes a gripping story for you and gets it back covered in red ink with the comment 'Spelling and handwriting need attention', (s)he is unlikely to try very hard the second time. You will need to work out how you are going to respond to spelling errors and how you might tie this in with any spelling programme a student is following. The same applies to your attitude to handwriting. Some dyslexic learners also experience the co-ordination difficulties of dyspraxia. Be prepared at an early stage in secondary school to stop worrying about handwriting and suggest that a student uses a laptop for written work. You will also need to consider the full potential of ICT support explored in Chapter 8.

PRACTICAL TASK PRACTICAL TASK PRACTICAL TASK PRACTICAL TASK PRACTICAL TASK

Find out if your school has a marking policy and, if so, what it is. If there is nothing in place, discuss with your mentor how he or she feels you should mark work. Consider what you have learnt about dyslexia. Do you agree with her suggestions?

Since writing is such a challenge for a dyslexic learner, you will need to consider whether you can use alternative forms of assessment, both to check if students have retained new information and to allow them to display their creativity and any outcomes of their research. You should discuss assessment opportunities with your mentor and consider allowing students to use posters, presentations, drama, workshops, discussions or any other forms of assessment. Get suggestions from your students too and consider using peer appraisal.

PRACTICAL TASK PRACTICAL TASK PRACTICAL TASK PRACTICAL TASK PRACTICAL TASK

In the staff room, talk to other teachers about how they assess students' knowledge and application and compile a list of possible ways you might try out.

Weak area 2: reading

You have already seen an example of what can happen when a student is asked to read out loud in a way that will expose his vulnerability. You will need to consider how you can deliver some materials to students who cannot read out loud or follow in a book when someone else reads.

Even if students have seemingly overcome some of their reading difficulties, they are likely to have to concentrate hard to read and understand and this is exhausting. You will need to think about how much reading you will require of them and why. There is the obvious argument that students need to practise reading skills to become fluent but is your difficult lesson on trigonometry the place to ask them to do this? Consider providing alternative support systems both within the lesson and for private study. These can include a study partner, TA, providing material on tape, ICT programmes. You should discuss with your mentor or the SENCo what provisions the school offers.

If you decide that it is essential for students to read worksheets or information, consider whether you need to provide differentiated worksheets. There are arguments for and against these in terms of labelling and stigma. You must also consider the size, colour and type of font and the colour of paper they are printed on. Some dyslexic learners suffer from difficulty processing print which is exacerbated by small-sized black type on white paper and can lead to eye strain and headaches. Some of your students will find coloured paper, coloured overlays or tinted glasses make a significant difference to the stability of the print. You should also look critically at your worksheets, text books and material photocopied from sources. What reading level is the language? How crammed is the page? How clear is the layout? Try to use clear, large print, leave space. There is no excuse for handwritten, cluttered worksheets. Leave out unnecessary reading and writing if you are not focussing upon these skills.

Find some exemplar worksheets from a range of teachers at your school, including one you had prepared earlier. Evaluate the extent to which they meet the dyslexia-friendly criteria provided above.

Weak area 3: speed of processing

Dyslexic students hate to be rushed (Johnson, 2004). So many tasks and assessments, particularly in mathematics, insist upon timed work. Consider carefully whether time is an important element of the skill you are testing or practising. If not, take the pressure off the dyslexic learners and let them complete at their own pace. In an ideal world, you would be able to take time to ensure that they finish work, that they are not pressured and that they are allowed breaks because they have to concentrate so hard on much academic work. Unfortunately, the world of the secondary school is not necessarily ideal.

Time management is difficult and it is a skill that experienced teachers take a long time to develop. You are concerned that your lesson cracks along at an energetic pace and that you cover all that the curriculum demands. It is so easy to lose students along the way. You will need to think carefully about how you will manage this for all those learners who work at different paces. Are you going to set a minimum number of learning aims and factor in extra activities for those who complete? Are you going to make use of TAs and divide the class into groups with different targets? Are you going to allocate maximum time for activities and stop the students, regardless of whether they have finished or not? There are no easy answers. Time management will need to be discussed with as many experienced teachers as possible and you are likely to try out many ways of dealing with it. The only factor that must not be forgotten is that most dyslexic learners work more slowly than their peers and frequently need to have new skills reinforced more intensively.

Weak area 4: remembering and organising

There is a fine line between supporting a student and rendering him or her helpless. You will be aware that many dyslexic learners have difficulties with organisation and memory. However, some of the most successful dyslexic public figures are obviously highly organised. This is usually because they have devised highly sophisticated systems to help them to cope. The environment of the dyslexia-friendly classroom should both avoid the stress caused by unnecessary chaos and poor organisation and model and foster strategies in the dyslexic learner. Your lesson activities need to be clearly structured and organised in such a way that any movement around the class is calm and orderly. You will also need to ensure that students work to develop ways of organising themselves. The classroom could contain many of the following to which you should bring students' attention.

- Clear, large print timetable, with colour-coded day identification. For example, Monday highlighted in yellow, Tuesday in blue, etc.
- Chart showing the days when specific items need to be brought.
- Map of school showing routes relevant to your students.
- Large topic map of course that you are following with a 'You are here' movable arrow.
- Clearly organised and labelled sets of resources such as pens, rubbers, etc. However, students should be encouraged to take responsibility for replacing them in the right places and not to assume that they can rely upon you. You should consider offering rewards for the students who manage to bring the right equipment rather than punishments for forgetting.
- Materials to help students to organise as described earlier in this chapter.

- Materials such as file dividers and plastic A4 envelopes to help students organise their work files. You might want to make time for some students to learn to organise their files with the help of a TA or a study-buddy.

Memory difficulties also have an impact upon students' ability to absorb information. Students are more likely to take in what they have been told if you ensure that they are in the best possible position to pay attention. You should make certain that a student with dyslexia sits facing the focus of the lesson and you need to ensure that you have his or her attention when you give instructions. These principles also apply to delivering curricular information where some dyslexic learners may find the sequencing or vocabulary of complex processes difficult to retain. You can use the learners' names to focus them or suggest an active listening strategy such as 'Stop, look at me and listen' which is employed whenever important instructions are about to be given.

When you are giving instructions, break them into short, grammatically simple parts and check that the class has understood each one before moving on. You can ask a member of the class to repeat the instructions back to you. Try to ensure that any student with attention difficulties does not feel afraid to admit he or she has missed something – many have been shouted at in the past for not paying attention – ensure also that they are aware that paying attention is a skill that you will help them to develop. So many students get into so much trouble simply because they misunderstand instructions.

Weak area 5: copying from the board

PRACTICAL TASK PRACTICAL TASK **PRACTICAL TASK** PRACTICAL TASK **PRACTICAL TASK**

Copy this accurately: You should be able to do this in 40 seconds.

Triyok vil ostropol vland groogour in triamfolon. Antraion plotor vil hlanda. Shry the vranfikon onf grrogour. Slaak vland rilton hak vil in frodorr.

How easy was that for you? Did it take 40 seconds? If it did, you are pretty impressive but you still need to think about what you had been asked to do. No doubt you kept having to look back at the panel to find out which word came next and how it was spelled. Did you find it easy to locate where you were each time? Did you feel pressured by the time? Did you think about what it meant? What skills do you have to use quickly and efficiently to do this effectively?

This is probably as close as it gets for you to experience what attempting to copy from the board might be like for a dyslexic learner who can only read parts of what is written up there.

Ground Rule

- Don't ask dyslexic students to copy from the board or a book. If they need the information, give it to them.

Weak area 6: giving vital lesson instructions

you will be surprised by the number of instructions which are given out to pupils in a lesson. Processing instructions puts pressure on those with weak memory skills and those who find sequencing information difficult. You must ensure that any instructions you give are clear and uncomplicated. You need to think carefully about the type of instructions you give during a lesson. These can range from instructions about:

- homework;
- tasks to be completed in the lesson;
- procedures and processes which are integral to your lesson.

The timing of your instructions is of vital importance for vulnerable learners. If you want your pupils to tackle their homework effectively, one of the ways of ensuring this is to give homework information at the beginning of your lesson when they are relatively fresh, and memories have not been overloaded with lots of subject information. Often newly-qualified teachers find that they run out of time at the end of a lesson and have not covered all aspects which were planned. Consequently, homework is given out as the bell goes and when the pupils are rushing to pack up and get to the next lesson. Noise levels are understandably high and for those with auditory processing difficulties, this is not conducive to taking down information accurately. Thus, giving out homework at the beginning of the lesson when noise levels are reduced will ensure that you provide the best environment for concentration; similarly, dyslexic pupils can be encouraged to record information in homework books or use alternative systems discussed earlier in the chapter.

If instructions contain an element of sequences and processes, you need to consider how best to provide this information for all your class. Large, clear, numbered points will help dyslexic learners to keep track of where they are in the process. TAs can be used effectively to provide 'task cards' for groups of pupils to follow when carrying out tasks and activities. As you gain experience, you will find that you use some activities and procedures frequently and can have such task cards prepared in advance.

PRACTICAL TASK PRACTICAL TASK **PRACTICAL TASK** PRACTICAL TASK **PRACTICAL TASK**

As part of your teaching practice observations, monitor the types and frequency of instructions given in a lesson. Note the teaching strategies used by experienced teachers to support vulnerable learners. See the example provided below.

Instruction	Frequency	Strategy
Homework	Twice: At beginning and end of lesson	Repetition to ensure understanding

A SUMMARY OF **KEY POINTS**

> The inclusive classroom should include all learners – activities which support learners with dyslexia will be appropriate for any vulnerable learners.
> The inclusive classroom is made up of the following two ingredients: people who understand the difficulties posed by some of the practices current in mainstream classrooms, and teaching approaches which aim to remove these barriers and personalise learning.

> Avoid overloading the areas that are undermined by SpLD/dyslexia, teach to strengths and support weaknesses.

MOVING *ON* > > > > > > MOVING *ON* > > > > > > MOVING *ON*

- Remember to check the reflective task on page 44.
- Compile a dyslexia-friendly classroom check-list. Then review the use of people and strategies. Find two examples of 'unfriendly practice'. What are they and what changes might you make? You will find out more about this in Chapter 11.

FURTHER READING FURTHER READING FURTHER READING FURTHER READING

BDA (2006) *Achieving dyslexia-friendly schools resource pack*. 5th Edition. Reading: BDA www.bdadyslexia.org.uk

Johnson, M, Peer, L and Phillips, S (2006) *Dyslexia-friendly teaching: A professional development pack*. Reading: BDA.

Price, G A (2007) 'Inclusion: Special educational needs'. In Ellis, V (ed.). 2nd Edition, *Learning and teaching in secondary schools*. Exeter: Learning Matters.

Reid, G (2005) *Dyslexia and inclusion: Classroom approaches for assessment, teaching and learning*. London: David Fulton.

Thomson, M (ed.) (2004) *Dyslexia: Perspectives for classroom practitioners*. Reading: BDA.

5
The dyslexic reader and writer and the secondary curriculum

Chapter objectives

By the end of this chapter you should:

- be able to answer, 'What is reading?' and know the basic model of reading development and where the dyslexic student may struggle within this model;
- be able to explain what reading *decoding* is and what it looks like in your classroom;
- know how to consider the choice of text books and texts in relation to reading ages and text illustrations;
- be able to suggest ways of supporting reading development in the classroom;
- be able to suggest ways of accessing the curriculum as a poor reader or non-reader;
- be able to explain the difference between secretarial and authorial writing skills;
- be able to suggest ways of supporting the development of writing skills;
- be able to suggest ways of giving feedback on students' written work.

This chapter addresses the following Professional Standards for QTS and Core:

Q10, Q17, Q23, C17, C18, C19, C26, C27, C29

Introduction

As you have discovered as a PGCE student or newly qualified teacher (NQT), there is so much to learn and read about on your journey to becoming a good teacher. So, if you have dipped into this chapter, and you are not a teacher of English then you deserve some praise and congratulations. You have understood that every teacher within the secondary school is responsible for developing all students' reading and writing abilities. Difficulties in reading and writing lie at the heart of behavioural dyslexic differences and this chapter seeks to explain these differences, and suggest ways in which you can support the development of literacy skills as well as reduce the impact of poor literacy skills on accessing the curriculum you have to offer.

PRACTICAL TASK PRACTICAL TASK PRACTICAL TASK PRACTICAL TASK PRACTICAL TASK

Do you consider that your subject area has a heavy dependence on reading or writing skills? Return to this activity at the end of the chapter to see if your views and thoughts have changed.

Within your own subject area list the types of reading that a student may be required to do.

Within your own subject area list the types of writing that a student may be required to do.

There are of course two ways of looking at your subject from the viewpoint of students with dyslexia. First, they may view your lessons as a place where the need for literacy skills is minimised and their other learning strengths can shine. In a timetable heavily dependent on the acquisition of good literacy skills, this comes as a welcome island of enjoyment in the day. Second, however, there are no subjects within the GCSE curriculum and examination system where the need for literacy skills does not arise. It must therefore be the responsibility of every teacher to a) support students in developing those skills and b) be aware of the impact of poor literacy skills on the lessons you have planned and how to minimise such impact.

Dyslexia and reading in the classroom

The basic model of reading development

In trying to unravel the reasons why some students struggle with reading, educators and researchers devise models of reading development. Before looking at two models of reading development in relation to dyslexia, you need to understand the difference between reading decoding and reading comprehension.

Reading decoding

The essence of reading decoding is the ability to use the alphabetic system of the language and to map the letter combinations of print (graphemes) on to the sounds (phonemes) used. This allows readers to work out how to read words that they have never seen before. You will have heard this referred to as the teaching of phonics. For example the word 'discombobulate' is not a word that one sees very often and, within the context of this piece of writing, you may have used decoding skills to read it. (If you did not, then read this non-word 'reaphogulation' to understand what decoding skills 'feel like'.)

As you have read in Chapter 1, most students with dyslexia have a phonological deficit and this severely affects their ability to decode. Whereas most students without dyslexia will have learned how to crack this code in the primary school, (The Rose Review (2006) highlighted the need to include the teaching of 'synthetic phonics' in the early years and beyond) students with dyslexia find the acquisition of these skills extremely difficult. They need to be taught, using structured, cumulative, multi-sensory techniques, and will almost certainly enter the secondary school without fully knowing how the English alphabetic code operates. For some, with severe dyslexia, they may never acquire these phonic skills to the point of functional literacy.

In addition, the English alphabetic code is a complex one; there are often several graphemes for one phoneme and more than one phoneme for a grapheme. This places additional burdens on students with dyslexia. For example, the vowel sound /a/ can use the following graphemes.

Graphemes for /a/	Example	Your example
ay	day	
a-e	make	
ai	rain	
a	apron	
eigh	weigh	
ey	grey	
ea	steak	

Look at the table on page 53 and see if you can add a further example of a word using each grapheme. To really challenge yourself try to use a subject specific word.

Reading comprehension

The true purpose of reading is not to decode the words, but to understand what is being read; this is termed 'reading comprehension'. Reading comprehension can be affected by many factors. For all students in the classroom this would include factors such as reading experience, life experiences, intellectual ability and language ability. For example, you may have been able to decode the word 'discombobulate' but not be aware of its meaning. In addition to the factors noted, students with dyslexia will also have their reading comprehension affected by their decoding abilities, their verbal memory difficulties and their processing speed difficulties.

Models of reading development

Below are two early, but still useful, models of reading development. In addition to readers in your classroom with dyslexia, all readers will fall somewhere within Gough and Tunmer's model, and a basic understanding of this will assist you in planning and supporting reading development.

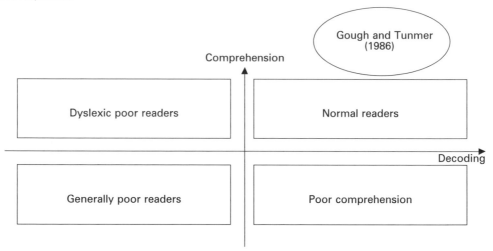

Figure 5.1 Models of reading development. Model adapted from Gough and Tunmer (1986)

Frith (1985) developed the 3-stage model of reading development. It explains how the reading process develops from early childhood to the adult fluent reader.

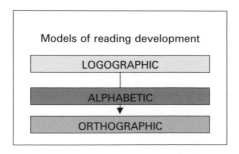

Figure 5.2 Reading development adapted from Frith (1985)

The Logographic Stage

In this first stage, words are recognised on the basis of a few crude visual features. This is a direct visual to verbal process. Learners make many errors and have no means of deciphering unfamiliar words. For example, they may be able to read their names. All words with the 'oo' pattern in them may be read as 'book'. Any long word may be read as 'hippopotamus' because their favourite bedtime story is called 'The Hippopotamus,' so they associate that with any written word that has a lot of letters. It is within this stage that young children start to recognise 'McDonald's signs, shopping carrier bag logos, favourite sweet wrappers and other familiar graphics.

The Alphabetic Stage

This is the stage where learners begin to utilise the alphabetic system to decode words. Links between the graphemes and phonemes are developed, as described above.

Orthographic Stage

This is the stage of fluent reading. There is an automatic recognition of printed words allowed by the amalgamation of logographic and alphabetic skills.

It is important to realise that these stages are not isolated, and one stage does not have to be completed before the learner can go on to the next stage. Thus, the learner who is a good reader may be functioning primarily in the orthographic stage but revert to the alphabetic stage for unfamiliar subject specific vocabulary.

Models of reading development will be affected by both behavioural factors (i.e. environmental Influences including educational opportunity) and cognitive and neurological factors within the individual (i.e. intellectual potential and/or specific learning difficulties, in this instance, dyslexia). However, you need to reflect on the following cycles. Educational opportunities will enhance cognitive and neurological development. Cognitive and neurological development will enhance educational opportunities. There is still some disagreement as to whether this movement occurs in both directions at the same time. In other words, are good readers destined to become even better readers due to being able to read more, which in turn enhances cognitive and neurological development, which in turn enables them to become better readers? Conversely are poor readers destined to stay poor readers?

So what do reading decoding difficulties look like in the classroom and how can you support them?

CASE STUDY

Cherry is in Year 10 and hates going to English lessons. At the moment they are studying *Dracula* and in order to read the novel the teacher is asking everyone to read round the class. Cherry starts to panic before going into the lesson. As soon as she has worked out in which direction round the class the teacher is calling on individuals to read aloud and how much she is expecting them each to read, Cherry spends the lesson trying to predict when her turn will be and what paragraph she is likely to have to read. She keeps her head down pretending to be following along, but instead reads her paragraph over and over in her head trying to decode the difficult words, particularly the characters' names. She is so intent on doing this that she never listens to what any other student is reading aloud. Cherry has been doing this every lesson since they started the novel, so Cherry has no idea of the story plot and has had no opportunity to follow along with the book to enjoy the content of the novel.

Countless students are placed in this position and react with exactly the same behaviour. Students with dyslexia should not be placed in this position. It damages their self-esteem and is counterproductive for you, the teacher. Never demand that a student with dyslexia reads aloud to the whole class. This includes short pieces of text, worksheets and notes on the white board. At best they will lose their respect for you. At the worst they will misbehave in order to save face and be removed from the classroom instead of being humiliated. Instead you could:

- Read to the students yourself. Think before insisting that students follow the text.
- Instigate a paired reading programme in your class. Students could/should choose their reading buddy. There are countless articles on paired reading.
- Instigate a 'volunteer' reading programme in your class. Students put their hand up when they wish to read. You choose the next three readers. They can read as little as one sentence and no more than one paragraph. When they want to stop reading they just say 'next' and the next reader takes over.
- Use unabridged tapes or CDs of novels for students to take home and 'read'.

You may be thinking, 'If they are not to read aloud, how else can I support reading decoding skills?' The following are some ideas that will help support you. Do make sure you add to the list any examples you observe of good teaching which encourage the development of decoding skills. Underline those that you already use, and select one or two of the new ideas as next steps for you.

1. Give all students a list of subject specific vocabulary at the beginning of each topic in alphabetical order. Make sure you give a copy of these to the teaching assistant in the class too.
2. Make explicit which words only need to be read, not spelt.
3. Liaise with the learning support department to share the list **before** you start the topic. Learning how to decode key words before the topic starts gives weak readers the time to over-learn the new words.
4. Write new words on the whiteboard, as you say them (they don't all look the way you say them). **Play with the word as you write it** – Split it into syllables, – note strange idiosyncrasies of the word. For example, 'There's **a rat** in sep**arat**e'. 'All enzymes in the digestive system end in the chunk "**ase**"', draw pictures within the word, e.g. turn the letter **o** into clock faces in words such as 'chr**o**n**o**logical',
5. Use starter sessions to practise key subject specific vocabulary. For example playing 'washing lines'. Selected students hold up single key words on a washing line (you may need to help them decode these), you read out a definition, students peg the definition onto the key word on the washing line. You can make whiteboard versions of this.
6. Put key words into PowerPoint. Use the audio recording and pictures to support decoding skills so that they see the word, hear it and have a picture of its meaning at the same time. This will help them store new words within a schema for easier retrieval (see Chapter 6). These will always make good revision tools later on.
7. Encourage the use of highlighter pens for key words on worksheets and test papers. In text books where this is not possible, use a clear acetate sheet and a paper clip over the page and highlight on that.

8. When reading texts, read out any words that have been **emboldened** or written in *italic* before reading the text.
9. On worksheets give lists of key words at the top.
10. Use 'read back' facilities as an IT tool when working on the computer. This can include cutting 'hard to decode' articles from the internet, and pasting them into Word where IT tools such as Text Help can read the text aloud to the student.
11. Select reading material that suits the students you are working with, in terms of reading age as well as interest.

Do not

1. Give key word lists as spelling homework.
2. Make fun of students who misread words due to decoding difficulties. (For example reading out 'mice' pies in a poem instead of 'mince' pies because the words look similar.)
3. Expect students to remember key words when they are revisited later on unless there have been opportunities for over-learning them as part of the learning process (see Chapter 6).

How to work out the reading age of a text

Due to these decoding difficulties it was noted in Chapter 3 that students with dyslexia are highly likely to have reading ages that are lower than their chronological age. In this section you will find out how to work out the reading age of texts. Before reading on, reflect on the following question.

PRACTICAL TASK PRACTICAL TASK **PRACTICAL TASK** PRACTICAL TASK **PRACTICAL TASK**

What is it within a piece of reading that gives it a high or low reading age?

There are several ways of working out the reading age of a text. The following is a simple quick method using the SMOG index. There are others, including IT tools that will do this for you. Just use a search engine to type in 'reading ages'.

Calculating the SMOG level of a text
(**S**implified **M**easure **o**f **G**obbledygook)

1. Select a page of a book.
2. Count 10 sentences.
3. Count the number of words which have three or more syllables.
4. Multiply this by three.
5. Circle the number closest to your answer.
   1 4 9 16 25 36 49 64 81 100 121 144
6. Find the square root of the number you circled.
   1 4 9 16 25 36 49 64 81 100 121 144
   1 2 3 4 5 6 7 8 9 10 11 12
7. Add 8 to that number. This will be the reading age.

The SMOG level of readability is quite simple to calculate (although using a calculator can help if you wish). The SMOG also suggests a readability based on 100% comprehension. So, if the text has a SMOG readability of ten, then the average ten year old, with an average reading ability, would be able to understand **all** of it.

For example:

Ten sentences contained 78 words with three syllables or more.
The nearest number is 81.
Its square root is 9. Add 8 = 17. The text would have a readability of 17.
(A reading age of 17 is high.)

PRACTICAL TASK PRACTICAL TASK PRACTICAL TASK PRACTICAL TASK PRACTICAL TASK

Select a text book you use and work out its reading age. By now you may have realised that the reading age of a text depends on two factors.

- The length of the sentences.
- The length of the words within those sentences.

So, when selecting texts for groups of students, particularly articles from the web, do consider both these points.

A further method using Microsoft Word is included in the Appendix 2.

Reading skills

It was noted earlier that there are three difficulties students with dyslexia face which impact on reading comprehension: decoding, memory difficulties and processing speed difficulties. In order to minimise this impact do ensure that you are aware of the following different reading skills, and make conscious efforts to model these skills to students whenever appropriate to encourage them to be metacognitive about their strategies.

Skimming

Reading headings, sub headings, and key first sentences in paragraphs to 'get the gist' of an article. Using highlighter pens as part of this exercise will support students in comprehending what they are about to read. You need to model good skimming skills in the classroom, before any text is read. (For further detail read Chapter 8.)

Scanning

Finding a specific word, number, name or instruction within a text. This does not involve reading closely but using your eyes to scan quickly for visual clues, such as capital letters, chunks of the word, signs and symbols. It should be quick. Today's students appear to have highly developed scanning skills, including students with dyslexia.

Close reading

Required for exam questions, following instructions, fire notices, etc. Every word needs to be read carefully. Some words need to be understood within the **CONTEXT** of the text. For example 'Look at the **illustration** below.' '**Illustrate** your answer.' In close reading you may need to distinguish between relevant and irrelevant information – 40% of adults cannot read and act on a hotel fire notice because they do not practise the skill of close reading.

Reading for pleasure

This is private reading. Texts can be chosen that are too easy, or too difficult. It is not necessary to understand everything or read correctly every word that is read. Chunks can be missed out. You are not required to remember the detail of every paragraph. Often reading for pleasure involves reading aloud to others, sharing the content and re-reading texts you already know. Reading for pleasure is something that students with dyslexia are unlikely to undertake. However, to help them, they need to be made aware of, and have practice in using, the other reading skills described above.

Finally, students with dyslexia often need to read a text at least twice; once to decode it, and then a second time to comprehend it. Therefore they are often given additional time in examinations. Give time and opportunities for this in your classroom.

A caution

Above all think carefully about the amount and quality of reading required in your lesson (and what lesson they have before yours on the timetable).

First, ask yourself the question, 'Is it really necessary?' when setting a reading task.

Then:

Is there a fun way of ensuring this is read as groups or a whole class?
Have I planned the use of my support assistant to help when there is a heavy reading load?
Have I considered the decoding needs and comprehension needs of my students?
Have I used all available IT to support my readers by:

1. choosing a reader-friendly font for work sheets, PowerPoint, etc. (Comic Sans MS and Arial are considered easier to read for students with dyslexia);
2. using free downloadable resources to allow the background colour on screens to be changed (e.g. Colour-Explorer.exe via www.microlinkpc.co.uk). Some students with dyslexia also have a condition known as Scotopic Sensitivity Syndrome or Irlen syndrome, and coloured lenses or different coloured backgrounds for reading text helps to alleviate the symptoms of eye strain, text jumping around or forming 'rivers' on the page causing eye rubbing headaches;
3. using text to speech software;
4. checking that any illustrations or graphics are used well to support the key words;
5. checking that your handwriting is readable on the whiteboard;
6. checking that written comments back to students are legible and in words that are easy to decode?

The dyslexic writer in the classroom

If you were to ask most students with dyslexia which they find more difficult, reading or writing, the majority would select writing. As students progress through secondary school, writing skills become more complex for everyone. For students with dyslexia the cognitive differences they possess compound this, by adding:

- spelling difficulties;
- handwriting difficulties;
- word finding difficulties;

- sequencing skill difficulties;
- organisational skills difficulties.

However, students with dyslexia are not the only students who struggle with some of these difficulties, and so the support you offer in the classroom will benefit your entire class.

Writing skills can be subdivided into two sets of skills; secretarial skills and authorial skills. Before looking at the list below, brainstorm some for yourself by reflecting on the writing skills you have required of students this week and whether they were secretarial or authorial skills.

PRACTICAL TASK PRACTICAL TASK PRACTICAL TASK PRACTICAL TASK PRACTICAL TASK

Select a writing task from your area of the curriculum.

List the writing skills and highlight them as either authorial or secretarial.

Are you clear as to the difference?

There are several ways of supporting **secretarial** skills.

- Find out and adhere to your school's whole school spelling policy. If one is not in place, find out why not, and ask the Head of English and your HoD to set up a working party to produce one. (Use the BDA's Dyslexia-Friendly Schools Initiative to support you.)

- Do not say to a student, 'Don't worry about the spelling. I am interested in the content.' They do worry about the spelling – it gets in the way of their creativity and authorial skills. It is like asking a learner driver not to worry about the gear changes and concentrate on reading the road. Instead say, 'Try to use rich vocabulary and the key word lists. I won't be marking for your spelling and grammar errors.'

- Find out about the whole school marking policy. How does the school you work in acknowledge effort as well as content for written homework and class work? If there is no whole school policy, discuss this with your HoD so that at least you have a department policy to support you as an NQT.

- Use 'timed and signed' strategies in student homework organisers, so that you become aware of how long it takes individual students to produce free writing. Parents sign the organiser to verify the amount of time a student has spent on their homework. Inequitable time spent on completing homework due to writing difficulties for students with dyslexia is of great concern to most parents.

- Reduce the amount of copying that students are required to do. The challenge is to make your own classroom a 'copying-free' zone. Of course students need to have information and evidence in their books and folders, and to write in order to demonstrate evidence of their learning. Instead of copying, use quizzes, such as free software like 'hot potatoes' (www.halfbakedsoftware.com), or Cloze proce-dures. Copying is the lowest grade thinking task you can ask of a student, so good teachers should avoid it. However, if it is essential, use two different coloured whiteboard pens and alternate the colours of the lines to be copied. In this way students with weak spelling (and decoding) skills can keep track of their place and will find the task less onerous. But be prepared for chatting and disruption!

- Ask students to read their work aloud to a friend (chosen by them) so that they can hear where the punctuation needs to go.

- Be open to allowing students to use as many IT and technical aids as possible. This includes spell checkers, mind mapping software, text to speech software and speech to text software such as Dragon Dictate Naturally Speaking which releases students from the secretarial skills of writing and places the emphasis on the students' authorial skills in word programmes. This is not cheating, but in some schools students are made to feel that it is.

Supporting **authorial** skills is much harder, but improving these with students can give you the most satisfaction. As a newly qualified teacher your role will be to understand the types of writing activities required of students in your subject, and to ensure that when you set writing tasks you are aware of the types of writing you have asked for. Chapter 6 offers guidance in the range of types required across the curriculum.

The Key Stage 3 National Strategy Framework for teaching English (DfEE, 2001) divides the writing that students are required to study in English into four categories of writing triplets. These categories make an extremely good starting point in helping you to recognise and support writing activities. They are not only useful for English but also as a framework for writing across all subject areas. They are writing to:

1. imagine, explore and entertain;
2. explain and describe;
3. persuade, argue and advise;
4. analyse, review and comment.

REFLECTIVE TASK

Reflect on which categories of writing your subject uses and what the writing in this category 'looks like'.

CASE STUDY

For his homework Jarret has been asked to write a newspaper article for the day after Thomas Becket was killed. The teacher has supported Jarret with some excellent notes on key facts of the events leading up to Thomas's death and the killing itself. He has a time line of events with pictures, his key word lists and in class students were put into groups as reporters and witnesses to design interviews developing their thinking about the events orally. But the teacher, in attempting to make the homework more interesting to complete, has not given guidance on how to write in the style of a newspaper. Jarret arrives at lunchtime homework club in the learning support department to seek help in planning his homework. He says, 'I just need help planning what I want to write. I'll do that and then worry about putting it into a newspaper later on Dragon Dictate.' But to be successful Jarret needs to plan the writing style alongside the content. What does that style look like?

- Newspapers can explain, describe, argue but also must entertain. What is required in this homework?
- Newspapers have headlines (often exaggerated) and subheadings.
- Newspapers are written in columns.
- The 6 ws of **w**ho, **w**here, **w**hat, **w**hen, **w**hy and ho**w** are used to ensure the main ideas are covered in the first two paragraphs to keep the reader interested.
- Newspapers use quotes from bystanders to cover opinions as well as facts.

Once Jarret has been given these key points, a writing frame of the 6ws to plan the order in which he wishes to present the events, and chosen which points he will use as quotes, he is ready to complete the task effectively, using his IT tools to support his secretarial skills.

All students with dyslexia will need support in developing writing skills. You can help by:

- Giving writing frames – but make sure students become metacognitve about these so that they can transfer the skills learned from a writing frame to other areas of your subject and the curriculum.
- Keeping a folder of examples of model answers at different levels of ability for each topic to share with students. (We all want to know what the finished article should look like before we start. This is not cheating.)
- Allowing students choice in how they demonstrate their learning using:
  1. mind maps;
  2. bullet points;
  3. cloze procedures to complete;
  4. PowerPoints;
  5. designing questions to ask instead of answers;
  6. highlighting key facts and or sentences from texts and cutting and pasting these into their books;
  7. allowing a parent or teaching assistant to act as 'secretary' for an extended piece of writing;
  8. Using speech to text software.
- Do not ask students to make notes while watching a video unless you use a writing frame to guide their note making.
- Do not ask students to research a topic on the internet without giving guidance on sites which you have checked for suitability in terms of reading decoding and comprehension suitability.

Once students have produced a piece of written work do ensure that you give feedback to them as soon as possible. Otherwise they will have forgotten what they wrote about and the feedback will be useless. Realistically, this means reducing the amount of written work you ask for, so that you do not sink under a mountain of marking that is useless to the student with dyslexia. When giving feedback use the feedback Sandwich (Dupree, 2005):

- write something that was good about the work and link this to the grade if necessary;
- write one helpful comment to guide students in improving the work, again linking it to the next grade above the work if necessary;
- write another positive comment about the work.

A SUMMARY OF **KEY POINTS**

This chapter has covered the extensive topics of reading and writing together with the barriers to learning that these underdeveloped skills can lead to in students with dyslexia. By understanding the skills that underpin effortless reading and writing, together with the cognitive and behavioural reasons why students with dyslexia find the acquisition of literacy skills difficult, you can use the ideas within this chapter to ensure a more dyslexia-friendly working environment.

MOVING *ON* > > > > > > **MOVING** *ON* > > > > > > **MOVING** *ON*

REFLECTIVE TASK
REFLECTIVE TASK

Return to the answers you gave at the beginning of the chapter in the Practical Task. In what ways would you change the responses you gave?

List two concepts, ideas, suggestions from this chapter that you already carry out as part of your current teaching ASK (attributes, skills, knowledge). Select one new suggestion from the chapter and review and reflect on its implementation as part of your teaching.

FURTHER READING FURTHER READING FURTHER READING FURTHER READING

Dupree, J (2005) *Help students improve their study skills*. London: David Fulton.

Mortimore, T (2008) *Dyslexia and learning style: A practitioner's Handbook*. 2nd edition. Chichester: Wiley.

Ott, P (2007) *Teaching children with dyslexia. A practical guide*. Abingdon: Routledge.

Townend, J and Walker, J (2006) *Structure of language: Spoken and written English*. London: Whurr Publishers.

6
Personalising the teaching and learning environment across the curriculum

Chapter objectives

By the end of this chapter you should:

- be able to apply all that you have learnt so far to the full range of the secondary school curriculum;
- be able to offer the very best learning situation to any learner in your class with dyslexic type difficulties;
- understand more about specialist subject areas and how students can be offered ways to deal with the special demands that they make.

This chapter will target the following Professional Standards for QTS and Core:

Q10, Q11, Q12, Q17, Q26, C31, C32, C33, C35, C37a

Introduction

The development of literacy and support for vulnerable learners is no longer seen as the province of the English or 'special needs' departments. Within the inclusive school all subject specialists have their part to play in helping learners to access their field. Don't forget that the types of strategies that make life easier for learners with dyslexia will help a range of the more vulnerable children in your groups, which will lead to less stressful times for everyone.

The previous five chapters have examined the theory underpinning SpLD/dyslexia. They have suggested a number of ways in which dyslexia might affect a learner's behaviour, and the types of indicators that might lead you to suspect dyslexia. Suggestions have been made as to how a classroom can become dyslexia-friendly and a detailed discussion provided of ways in which literacy can be supported.

The emphasis so far has been upon the difficulties that accompany SpLD/dyslexia – understandably as the curricular focus has been upon the field of literacy, which tends to be challenging for these students. Outside this arena, however, learners with dyslexia can demonstrate a broad range of understanding and talent which boosts their self-esteem and their status as learners in the eyes of other students. Offered the right support, students with dyslexia are shown flourishing on higher education courses from mathematics, astrophysics, engineering and medicine to fine art, archaeology and performing arts (Mortimore, 2006). They need, however, to be given the chance to shine rather than to be restricted by the difficulties they frequently experience in the 'secretarial' aspects of the different subjects. How can this be done?

You will need to develop the following.

- Opportunities for them to show their knowledge, which is often surprising.
- Multi-media ways of circumventing the barriers set up by text.
- Clear descriptions of the types of written structures expected.
- Sensitivity to the types of language and sentence structure you are using when explaining or giving instructions. They need to be clear, simple, short and repeated.
- Differentiation by type of task, outcome and support offered (Reid, 2005).

Subject demands

All subjects bring specific conventions, structures and expectations. These can sometimes be termed 'schema'. A schema can refer to a student's expectations as to a topic or ways of working. One example of a schema is the set structure required when a student reports upon a biology experiment or organises an essay discussing an issue in history. Chapter 5 discussed the conventions or schema required by a newspaper article. All students need to be shown these conventions explicitly. You cannot expect the majority of learners, with or without SpLD/dyslexia, to pick these things up instinctively. All subjects will also contain specialist vocabulary or, at least, confusing words such as 'take away' in mathematics or 'current' in science, which can have multiple meanings, an everyday one and a subject specific one. Remember from Chapter 5 that these vocabulary terms must be introduced in advance and reinforced as they occur if vulnerable learners with any type of speech and language deficit are not to be lost.

As a subject teacher, it is important for you to examine the specific demands posed by your subject. Learning in any context or subject involves three interlinked stages.

- Getting the information in – modes of presentation.
- Processing the information – storing and revising.
- Getting the information out – modes of expression.

Each of these makes different demands upon the learner. Frequently learners with dyslexia will have difficulties at one or all of these stages.

Getting information in? How do students obtain information? Through reading, listening, watching, doing. You may have come across the concept of individual learning style preferences (Riding and Rayner, 1998; Reid, 2003; Mortimore, 2008). If so, you will understand that individuals tend to have particular preferences for, or difficulties with, specific types of processing. Some people may find it easier to absorb information if it is reinforced with images, as in a video, others will find learning through carrying out a procedure – trial and error – is the best way for them. Some may be happiest learning through the auditory or verbal channel alone, while their friends find that the easiest way to understand is to read silently. Some like to process information sequentially and respond to lists and logical order. Others prefer a big picture or concept map of a topic. You should also not forget the part played in successful learning by the emotions which are likely to be affected by a number of things. Dunn and Dunn (1991) suggest five domains which can influence the performance and attitude of vulnerable learners. These include the following.

- The learning environment (e.g. Do they prefer light, listening to music, solitude?).
- The emotional (e.g. Does stress or pressure inhibit or encourage them?).

- The sociological (e.g. Do they prefer to work individually, collaboratively, in teams, with a partner?).
- The physiological (e.g. At what time of day are they most alert? Do they need to be mobile? Able to eat?).
- The psychological (e.g. Are they likely to prefer sequential or big picture approaches? Do they favour visual or verbal processing?).

It is important to remember that every learner is an individual and needs to be encouraged to consider his or her own preferences so that a choice can be made of the most appropriate type of strategy for the individual and context and also to help the learner to select the best ways of working at home. When working with vulnerable learners, flexibility and the offer of a range of acceptable ways of achieving the goal are the keys to success.

Learners with SpLD/dyslexia may have difficulties with literacy; some will find it hard to focus and listen consistently; others will need ways of backing up their unreliable memories. It is important, however, not to assume that dyslexic students are likely to be visual learners who do not respond to verbal presentation. Experience and research suggest that multi-sensory methods are the most successful ways of developing literacy for learners with dyslexia and many also find that they are more receptive to information delivered in a multi-modal way. However, not everyone likes this way of learning and some just feel overloaded. The application of style theory to classrooms has recently come in for heavy criticism (Coffield et al., 2004); however, Mortimore (2008) and Reid (2005) describe a range of practical ways in which success can be fostered at all three stages of learning by the use of style preferences. Some of the strategies described in Chapter 8 on Study Skills relate to this approach to learning.

You will need to consider what demands are made by your particular subject at these three stages and then identify your most common ways of dealing with each. For example, for **stage one**, getting information in, if your students are expected to carry out independent research as a way of obtaining information, are sources provided in a multi-media form or is success dependent on their being able to find their way around a set textbook and read the print? Chapter 5 reminded you that you need to be aware of the reading level of the text or worksheet. (Now that you understand the criteria for readability levels – syllable and sentence length – you will find a quick way of checking the readability of any text you create using Word in Appendix 2.) Do you use websites? If so, how accessible are they? Can a student programme his laptop to enable the web page to be read to him? Are students expected to take notes? If so, have they been shown different ways of doing this and been helped to choose the way that suits them best? Chapter 8 provides some alternative ways of doing this.

At **stage two**, storing and revising the information, you are asking students to process and think about what they have found. This is often the planning stage and many students will happily ignore it, to their cost. You will find general advice on how to use writing frames and structures in Chapters 5 or 8. What is the task? Is it problem solving? Is it compare and contrast? Is it using information as evidence to answer a question? Are students learning French vocabulary off by heart? Do they understand the wording of the instructions? In a mathematics task, can they convert a real life problem into the mathematics activity they are meant to be practising?

Stage three usually results in a product of some sort based upon stages one and two. Frequently it is a piece of written work. Students with dyslexia usually find a blank page totally intimidating and will need some sort of framework to get them started. David Wray has produced some helpful writing frames which span the curriculum and explore the different schema attached to the different types of writing described in Chapter 5. Visit his website on http://www.warwick.ac.uk/staff/D.J.Wray/index.html

These frames can be adapted to be subject specific and help your students to structure and organise written responses. However, many who do manage to write an acceptable response realise that any written piece is only a shadow of what they actually know. The few who produce a detailed, accurately spelled piece have usually spent twice as long as their peers getting it right, which probably means some other task or homework subject will have suffered. You do need to consider exactly why you are asking for a written piece. Would some other way of demonstrating their knowledge be acceptable, perhaps a poster presentation, a taped piece, a chaired discussion? If a written piece is essential, does it need to be completely accurate as far as spelling and punctuation are concerned? Is there a role to be played here by a scribe or proofreader?

These questions refer to nearly all curriculum subjects, even art where eventually the student must write about the processes he or she has gone through. You will need to be clear as to the expectations of your subject and how they might pressurise students with SpLD/dyslexia. In general the problem areas are likely to be the following:

- literacy (especially written expression);
- organisation and structure;
- sequencing skills;
- memory.

This practical task requires you to consider your subject and to what extent the content, modes of delivery and assessment make demands upon these vulnerable areas.

PRACTICAL TASK PRACTICAL TASK **PRACTICAL TASK** PRACTICAL TASK **PRACTICAL TASK**

Think about your own subject.

Subject:

General skills needed:

How do you expect students to obtain information, carry out research?

Is there a particular terminology/vocabulary/convention?

Are particular formats required for writing (e.g. experiment)? If yes, what sorts?

What are the assessment demands? Examination? Practical task? Course work?

What specific demands are made upon:

- organisation and structure?

- sequencing skills?

- memory?

When you have completed this box, discuss it with a colleague from the same subject area and/or with the SENCo or your mentor. You will find further suggestions in the relevant subject sections within this chapter.

Working with specific subjects

The rest of this chapter provides some basic ideas to help you within your specific curriculum area. Each section will look at the extent to which the subject impinges upon areas of strength and weakness exhibited by learners with SpLD/dyslexia and will suggest some ways in which to support them. Literacy has already been covered in Chapter 5, mathematics will be explored in Chapter 7, and you have considered the extent to which your subject made demands upon literacy. You should now think about how you might dismantle any barriers to access caused by literacy difficulties and identify the other demands made by your subject. We would argue that no subject should be considered an exclusion area for people with literacy difficulties – after all Shakespeare did not write his plays to be read but to be performed, watched, enjoyed and discussed.

Activities

A selection of case studies is presented to enable you to suggest ways in which you might support these individuals within your area. You should also select a student from your class and devise appropriate in-class support for him or her.

Peer and Reid (2001) provide a series of chapters devoted to supporting students with SpLD/dyslexia across specific subject areas. The British Dyslexia Association has, in association with David Fulton, also published a series of practical and accessible books to help subject specialists accommodate learners with dyslexia. These include English, music, mathematics, ICT, design and technology, drama, modern foreign languages, PE, and others are in the pipeline. These all offer more detail for the individual specialist than it is possible to include here. Griffiths (2002), Cogan and Flecker (2004), Dupree (2005) and Mortimore (2008) provide a range of strategies for supporting students across the curriculum.

Remember for all subjects:

- reduce or compensate for the demands on literacy;
- make all tasks, technical schema and expectations clear. Provide structures and scaffold or model the process of developing written work;
- provide appropriate vocabulary;
- make your teaching as multi-sensory as you can;
- give vulnerable learners the opportunity to show and share their knowledge;
- avoid copying notes from the board wherever possible (provide notes if essential);
- reward positive behaviour.

Working with students in the humanities

Many of the challenges and suggested strategies are effective across all humanities subjects which tend to involve the reading, processing and writing of much factual material. Practical task 1 gave you the opportunity to consider the specific challenges of your subject and you may have come up with ideas that are not covered here.

English literature

A distinction must be made between English language and English literature, despite the fact that the UK English Language GCSE examinations currently require study of Shakespeare, poetry and a selection of literature. Within your English language teaching, there has to be an emphasis upon the building of basic literacy skills (see Chapter 5) as this is being evaluated. Within your literature teaching, however, the emphasis can be upon developing the student's sensitivity to ideas and themes and ability to discuss and express them. Students are likely to qualify for amanuenses or scribes, or to be able to use voice recognition software, and your goal should be to enable them to develop and show their insight and knowledge by offering access to the set texts in ways where their difficulties with basic literacy will not restrict them overmuch. It is often the case that a student who struggles to gain a C grade in English Language is capable of a B or higher in Literature.

Literacy (especially written expression) See also Chapter 5.

- Offer opportunity to bypass text where possible by reading to the students, providing recorded sections of the books, utilising computer software such as TextHelp to support them if they have to read sections independently. Focus in detail on short selected sections of text when, for example, studying Shakespeare.
- Make all possible use of oral strategies such as hot seating interviews, role play, dramatisation. Many students with SpLD/dyslexia are extremely fluent orally. Utilise group work where dyslexic students with creative ideas can be supported and in their turn support less imaginative students who do not have the same difficulties with writing.
- Train all students in note taking strategies (see Chapter 8) to enable them to capture key words and concepts. Many will make good use of mind or concept maps with visual icons, if encouraged to do so. To reduce the load on writing or note taking, which remains one of the most challenging skills for adults with dyslexia (Mortimore and Crozier, 2006), make use of interactive whiteboards to build up 'mind maps' of material and thoughts during lessons and then download these maps or place them on the wall for the students to access.

Organisation and structure

- Students will need to be taught explicitly how to recognise and reproduce the structures of stories and other types of writing. This will help them to analyse and criticise texts but also to structure their own. Some frames are provided in other chapters of this book. Two specific structures, a time line grid and the story chain Situation Problem Solution Outcome (SPSO), which are particularly useful for literature but also relate to other subjects, are provided in the Appendices (4 and 3). Students should be shown how to pick out the key words in any task or examination question and to structure a writing frame to suit it. They also need to be clearly aware of the marking criteria for particular types of course or examination work.
- Think carefully about how often you need to get a student with dyslexia to produce a neat, proofread copy of his or her work. A first draft will have taken a long time to produce unless you encourage students to present first drafts in note form as a plan. Remember the distinction between authorial and secretarial skills. Forcing a student at this point to be a secretary when he or she cannot recognise spelling or punctuation errors can often be a last straw. Do encourage students to make use of ICT wherever possible. Voice recognition software (see Chapter 8) can be used in a variety of ways – one way is to use it at the proof reading stage when the ideas have been captured and the student can talk them into the machine.

Sequencing skills

- Studying literature will frequently involve the ability to spot and memorise sequences of events. Coleman and Buzan's (1999) *Teach Yourself Literature Guides* are highly recommended as they provide a number of ways in which grids or frames can be used to help with understanding and revision. Try methods such as:
  - providing students with a series of boxes or blank squares to fill with main events;
  - time-lines (see the exemplar time-line grid of the events in John Steinbeck's *Of Mice and Men*

provided in the Appendix 3);
- cycles to show links and cause and effect.

Memory

- You are beginning to help students with memory strategies if you enable them to develop the skill of seeing structure or shape within a seeming mass of facts and then provide them with clear, often visual, ways of recording these as a pattern, concept map, SPSO, time-line etc. Using icons that remind them of characters will also help. Memory strategies are discussed in Chapter 8 which provides study skills and exam techniques. However, you need to be sure that you encourage students to use these and that you make your teaching as varied and multi-sensory as you can. The worst possible strategy for a student with dyslexia (or, in fact, any vulnerable learner) is expecting them to take unassisted notes while you talk.

History

Until comparatively recently, it had been suggested that history, with its demands upon writing skills, was an unsuitable subject for vulnerable learners. However, there has rightly been a change in attitude with a more flexible creative approach to teaching methodology and a realisation that the study of history, if appropriately delivered, can develop speaking and listening skills alongside literacy (Dargie, 2001). Learners with SpLD/dyslexia are fascinated by the true life stories of history. You will also occasionally find that such learners also show some aspects of Asperger's syndrome where they will have an obsessive and detailed interest in some topic, such as tanks in the second world war. This frequently leads them to choose history and your task will be to attempt to help them to place their narrow interest within the broader canvas of topics covered in the syllabus.

The suggestions made for English literature in relation to literacy, organisation, sequencing and memory all apply here. History is ideally suited to a range of multi-modal ways of delivery. However, history offers further challenges to learners with dyslexia in that success is dependent on the student understanding and developing the conceptual language that underpins history and runs throughout the rich selection of sources, diaries, letters, newspaper reports, advertisements or Government Acts that a student will be expected to interpret and evaluate. The teacher will need to ensure that students develop the skills of selecting information and using the appropriate evidence to evaluate it.

Literacy (especially written expression)

- Use multi-modal resources wherever possible.
- Make all possible use of oral strategies, structured role play, dramatisation, paired work where students must check that a partner can explain topics and terminology (Dargie, 2001). Utilise tapes and CDs for revision. Develop the student's ability to provided a sustained and detailed oral response. This will be vital if he or she needs to practise using a scribe for examination purposes.
- Ensure that text is at an appropriate reading level or that strategies are in place to help a student with more complex pieces. Check that it is presented in a large font format so that quality does not impede reading. It is useful to highlight key phrases and to provide glossaries on the classroom wall so that students get used to them.
- Present technical vocabulary at the start of any topic and revisit it frequently. Ensure that students understand the differing requirements of instructions such as 'compare', 'evaluate', 'discuss' and the types of writing that will accompany them.

Organisation, structure and sequencing skills

- Learners with dyslexia are likely to need help with extracting the main structure of a narrative from extraneous detail and may often be overwhelmed by the extent of factual information provided.
- Offer systematic training in note taking strategies (see Chapter 8) which helps them to develop their own strategies and shorthand and makes them think about what suits their preferred way of memorising material. Provide clear revision notes which make use of as many graphic types of presentation as possible – use flow charts, Venn diagrams, keyword concept maps, time lines, etc. Ensure that students are asked to move information across different modes of expression (e.g. write out what the Venn diagram shows; put the sequence of events in the Normandy landings into a time-line).
- Provide appropriate writing frames with paragraph openings and key vocabulary. Practise creating these frames in response to examination tasks. Provide examples of responses to tasks and analyse why they are good or bad.
- Teach students how to interpret tasks and examination questions using a technique such as the BUG technique (Price, 2006, see Appendix 5).
- Be selective in your demand for technical accuracy. Make use of ICT and voice recognition software (see Chapter 8).
- Ensure that the student's history file is organised clearly and in sequence. Learners with SpLD/dyslexia may need a study buddy or classroom assistant to help them with this and it should be checked regularly.

Memory

- Remembering facts will be a challenge. You will need to provide clear revision notes as suggested above, plus audio cassettes/DVDs, plus much practice in applying information to particular examination questions.
- Ensuring that the history file is clearly organised and labelled will help.
- Make use of group study and study buddies.
- Try to ensure that students have to report back regularly on what they have learnt. You can suggest that they prepare a weekly mind map of information gained and share it with a friend as part of the start of the next week's lessons. This way, the information will be re-processed before it is forgotten.

Geography

Much of the advice offered for history on literacy, memory and organisation is equally relevant to geography. Learners with SpLD/dyslexia frequently relate well to geography. It is visual and directly relevant and they respond to the enquiry based, problem solving approach – provided that you have considered how to overcome literacy barriers and how to ensure that they know the expectations of each task or project. There will be technical vocabulary to teach and the challenge of field work organisation, projects and interviews.

Organisation

Field trips: be certain that all the appropriate permission letters get home! Ensure that the student has prepared the following things in advance of the day and that everything is in the back pack on the day – a study buddy can be helpful here.

- Break the project into its component parts and ensure that an itemised list of what needs to be done, and when, is glued into a relevant file/diary
- Consider whether field notes need to be taken and how this might be done – Dictaphone? Scribe?
- Consider how the student will store and analyse raw data
- Ensure that the student has all the equipment needed
- Ensure that the student has remembered where you are meeting, at what time, etc.

Memory

- The student with SpLD/dyslexia will need much help with revising for exams and also understanding exactly what the different examination questions require. See the history suggestions here and the BUG technique and ensure that multi-media is used in the presentation of information whenever possible.
- It has been suggested that students with dyslexia often see how individual sets of data relate with each other to comprise the 'big picture'. This is not necessarily the case (Mortimore, 2008) and the provision of 'big picture' maps on classroom walls, to show how things fit together, is likely to help all the learners in your groups.

Modern foreign languages

Debate is ongoing as to whether students with SpLD/dyslexia should be made to study a foreign language. It could be argued that this is yet another way of reducing opportunity and certainly, both outside the UK and for immigrants inside the UK, developing the ability to speak English can be crucial for educational and career progress. It is, however, important to be aware that students with SpLD/dyslexia will have to work harder than others to be successful (Crombie and McColl, 2001) and that the difficulties any learner with dyslexia has in the native language will affect the ability to absorb another language. If the learner can choose which language to study, it is probably better to choose one that is close in structure/ pattern to the native language. This book does not deal directly with the support of learners for whom English is an additional language. However, the strategies suggested will be vital for them and, if you have these students within your classroom, suggestions for their support will be found in the collection edited by Peer and Reid (2000).

Students who find phonological processing difficult in English will also flounder in French or German if teaching relies overmuch upon auditory processing without specific teaching of the phoneme–grapheme linkages in the relevant language. Teachers of modern foreign languages should look carefully at all the suggestions offered in Chapter 5 for teaching the native language, as these will be equally appropriate for the learning of a second language. It is suggested that a range of learners will respond to the structured, sequential, reinforced way of introducing patterns within language through the use of multi-sensory techniques (listening/speaking/reading/writing) which utilise all the senses simultaneously. Research (Downey and Snyder, 1999) suggests that you need to cut down the amount of content you cover and teach this core in a highly structured, multi-sensory way.

Memory

MFL makes heavy demands upon memorisation.

- Select key vocabulary, group it logically – by pattern, theme, gender – and set **short** sets for memorisation frequently rather than long lists intermittently.
- Use all the memory strategies suggested in Chapter 8 or by Dupree (2005) or Mortimore (2008).
- The more you can make use of multi-sensory strategies – cue cards, games, colour, ICT, mime, gesture – the more will be retained.

Media studies

Students with SpLD/dyslexia frequently flourish in this area, particularly if the focus is upon visual/graphic media. Many, but by no means all, seem to have a strong sense of visual narrative and, when offered appropriate structures such as storyboards, enjoy analysing shots and sequences and explaining why such techniques are effective. This is also often a way into literary criticism (see Mortimore, 2008) and can have a knock on effect in helping to develop ways of revising information (present the stages in the scientific experiment as a storyboard). They will all, however, need specific structures and frames to help them analyse and report back and to develop course work and all the suggestions made in the humanities section, in particular those for English literature, are likely to be relevant here.

PRACTICAL TASK PRACTICAL TASK **PRACTICAL TASK** PRACTICAL TASK **PRACTICAL TASK**

Humanities: How would you support these students?

Case Study One: Profile

Jenny is eleven years old and in Year 7. She has been diagnosed as dyslexic. She has many difficulties with phonological processing and tends to depend upon whole word strategies plus analogy and rhyme. She is of average ability with talents in art and practical subjects. She works very hard and can become discouraged when she finds it difficult to express what she knows on paper. How might you help her to contribute effectively to a relevant project within your subject area?

Case Study Two: Select a student in one of your groups who is struggling.

Your student:

Profile

How would you support him or her?

Working with students in the sciences

In our experience of supporting students across the curriculum, after mathematics, science is the most common area where help is sought. Science is an area where dyslexic learners can shine as there is less emphasis upon writing and information is frequently gleaned through experience, observation or video. The fact that it is suggested that Einstein did not learn to read fluently until he was nine, and that he admitted to having real difficulties with words, shows how fluent literacy does not need to be a barrier! Frequently the students are interested in science and follow the ideas so this is not an issue of lack of motivation or ability.

However, there is much to challenge the learner with SpLD/dyslexia in this area. Much of physics is underpinned by mathematics which may in itself be a learner's weakness. There is specific and sometimes ambiguous vocabulary (I thought currents came in buns) which must be provided and taught, and the need to learn facts and labels (e.g. symbols for the periodic table). Hunter (2001) suggests that you need to consider how you conduct your group work to enable the frequently disorganised, dyslexic learner to juggle booklets, apparatus and note-making while attempting to listen to the teacher to whom his back is turned! Consider how you place the student and with whom; how you can issue a clear plan for the session in advance; how you might provide a grid or blank word frame upon which the student can record data as things progress. Again, it is a matter of analysing the task you are setting into its components and providing support structures.

Always think clearly about how you expect the student to record information. Note-taking is one of the longest lasting difficulties described by adult students in higher education (Mortimore and Crozier, 2006) yet school children are often expected to write notes from dictation or to make their own while watching a video. Teachers then wonder why their understanding and recall seems to be so poor. You will need to provide frames and support strategies.

Organisation

- It is essential to help your students to organise their files or exercise books. Notes or information from each lesson must have a heading and a date. Some students may not remember what they were doing last week and how this week follows on from it. They need to be provided with the 'big picture' of the topic they are doing and how it all fits together to enable them to understand and recall. If lesson notes are not clearly labelled and organised in sequence, they can be difficult to learn and impossible to revise from six months later. It is worth spending time at the end of each week to pull things together and make sure that students check that their files are in order. Encouraging parents to co-operate in this will also be useful.
- Students will need help with organising the stages of any course work. You need explicitly to teach (and probably re-teach) the structure demanded by the 'write-up' in any experiment. See the SPSO framework in Appendix 4. This is a useful and simple framework to start a write-up.

Memory

Many students struggle with vocabulary, processes and chemical formulae. (See chapter 8's suggestions as to relevant study skills and examination strategies.) It is important to make everything as real and relevant to the student as possible, to use multi-modal ways of presenting and strategies such as concept mapping and unlabelled diagrams which they must label. The excellent subject support revision guides provided by the Science Co-ordination Group publications provide good examples (see, for instance, Parsons, 1997) although they do unfortunately date quickly. However, many of the pages are crammed with too much information for a vulnerable learner so you may want to isolate specific sections.

PRACTICAL TASK PRACTICAL TASK **PRACTICAL TASK** PRACTICAL TASK **PRACTICAL TASK**

Sciences: How would you support these students?

Case Study Three:

Profile

Sharon is studying AS level geology. She has been diagnosed with dyslexia. She is very interested and motivated and hopes to complete a degree in the subject. She has mild dyspraxia which affects her fine motor co-ordination and she finds using diagrams, charts or maps very difficult. Her reading is mostly compensated but involves a lot of effort. The group are about to go on a field trip to Tenerife and must plan a project related to volcanic and seismic activity. How would you prepare and support her?

Case Study Four: Select a student in one of your science groups who is struggling.

Your student:

Profile

How would you support him or her?

Working with students in the arts and sport

Many students with SpLD/dyslexia flourish in this aspect of the curriculum and go on to succeed at art school or within the world of performing arts or sport. Think of Keira Knightley, the actress, Steve Redgrave, the oarsman. This success can really raise a student's confidence and reputation. However, there are just as many students who are not talented in performing arts or sport and there is currently no evidence that dyslexia brings with it such talents. These are areas, however, where students are mostly less constrained by the written word than in other aspects of the curriculum so it is sometimes easier to succeed here. Being good at sport or drama or art can also be seen publicly as 'cool' which is a real boost to self-esteem. These subjects do, however, have their challenges for students with SpLD/dyslexia, particularly for those who go on to pursue them at higher education level, and they need to be prepared to encounter these.

So what are the challenges? With each subject, and also with PE, if students choose to take public examinations, there will come the point where the student has to analyse his or her experience in writing. Here, all the strategies offered across the humanities and sciences will be relevant. Students will need frames and structures, they will need to be introduced to vocabulary, shown how to memorise and revise. You may even find that they are particularly resistant to this aspect of the course, having perhaps selected it for its lack of pressure upon literacy! Each area also makes specific demands.

Art
Arguably this subject poses fewer challenges than most. Much of the learning is experiential, taught through demonstration and practice. However, there has been an increasing emphasis on conceptual development and explicit planning which some find hard to grasp. Some learners with SpLD do, of course, also experience dyspraxic type difficulties, and for them precision drawing or even dealing with equipment in a crowded art room can be hazardous. Others may have difficulties with concentration and attention, with listening to instructions when drawing or with remembering to bring equipment or leave time to clear up. Specific instructions will help here. Overall, however, the art room can be a place to shine for many, although it should not be forgotten how public the frustration of being a hopeless artist can be!

Design and technology
Design and technology (D&T) sometimes seems like a halfway house between science and art. Many students with SpLD/dyslexia have a real flair for the design and making of things. However, they can find the 'scientific' aspects frustrating. There are facts, terminology and processes to be learnt, carried out and recorded. There are also theoretical examinations to complete alongside coursework which has to be researched, timed, documented and organised. In fact many of the challenges of the sciences and the strategies suggested in this section apply to D&T. However experience suggests that some of the students who excel at the practical side of D&T find the language skills of the competent scientist elude them and they therefore struggle with this aspect. The structuring and explanation of course work projects can also pose a challenge. The exam will need to be revised for and students will need the usual support with problem solving, key words for questions and interpretation. They are likely also to need support with the technical vocabulary which they may find hard to read and with bridging the gap between the technical instructions given and the practical activities required.

Drama/dance/PE
Many articulate students with SpLD/dyslexia end up in the world of performing arts. Likewise many are excellent athletes. However, do not forget that the student with dyspraxia or with mild Asperger's syndrome or the person who is lost for words may well find these lessons humiliating. Being constantly mocked or in trouble because you cannot tie your trainer laces, spent 15 minutes getting changed or forgot your towel again, capped by being the last to be chosen for the teams every time is a killer. Some of these students will do anything to get out of these lessons.

There are challenges too for those who enjoy them.

- In **drama**, the overuse of scripts excludes those whose reading is poor and learning a part can need the support of technology or friends. Improvisation can be difficult if your word retrieval is effortful, if your mild Asperger's syndrome makes it impossible for you to imagine being in someone else's shoes or you feel threatened by the unpredictability of the lesson. Putting on a production offers a variety of roles which can be tailored to an individual's strengths and a range of groupings where students can support each other. However, the complexity of planning and timing which goes into a production will need careful analysis so that the dyslexic student retains what has to be done and when.
- **PE** involves being able to change quickly and efficiently into your kit which you remember to bring on the right day. It means understanding and remembering complex rules and procedures. It involves following oral instructions sometimes involving special terminology (anyone explain silly mid off?). It means being well co-ordinated, being able to 'read' a game and predict outcomes. It also demands a good sense of space, of where your body is within that space and from what direction a rather hard ball might come thundering towards you.
- In **dance** all of these apply and you have to be able to follow and retain sequences of movements, frequently shouted at you from the back of a hall. To cap it all, in ballet these usually have French names! All of this in public and usually at speed.

Think back to Chapter 2 and you will realise how many hazards there are here for a learner with SpLD/dyslexia and no particular athletic talent! Even if you are a natural runner or dancer, you may need help if these hazards are not to prevent you from showing your talent.

How can the teacher help students to master these challenges? Being aware that they exist and the impact that they can have upon self-concept and behaviour is a good start. You will need to develop your own particular strategies within the subject. Some of these challenges are unavoidable so the focus becomes how you deal with the student's failure without humiliating him or her. These are very public subjects where it is easy to feel exposed.

Music

Music offers wonderful opportunities for self expression and confidence. It is multi-sensory, can adapt to suit the performer's skills and preferences and has the potential to include everyone. There will, however, be some challenges for those learners with SpLD/dyslexia who do discover the musician within themselves and then want to become more skilled or specialised which will involve both practical and theoretical examinations. As always, these challenges tend to fall into the areas of literacy, organisation and memory. Ditchfield (2001) presents the main difficulties which include:

- reading music – differentiating between symbols; losing your place on a sheet of music; following sequences; sight reading at speed under pressure;
- eye–hand co-ordination;
- writing musical notation while composing;
- understanding of the theory and mathematical calculations that underpin notation and rhythm;
- memory, either for patterns and phrases or for the type of aural perception that is tested in exams;
- organisation – bringing equipment at the right time to the right class.

You will need to consider how you can make your teaching systematic and cumulative with as much multi-sensory reinforcement as possible. Make every use of computer technology (particularly in conjunction with a keyboard) for learning notation, theory, practice and composition. Try to discover your individual student's profile of strengths and weaknesses and match these with strategies.

PRACTICAL TASK PRACTICAL TASK **PRACTICAL TASK** PRACTICAL TASK **PRACTICAL TASK**

The Arts: How would you support these students?

Case Study Five:

Profile

Jonty is thirteen years old and in Year 9. He has severe literacy difficulties. He is a virtual non-reader and finds expressing his ideas in writing very hard. He comes from a farming family, is very involved with the animals and has a wide knowledge of practical issues related to his background. He is becoming anxious and depressed in school. He has become withdrawn and unwilling to participate. How might you encourage him in your subject?

Case Study Six: Select a student in one of your arts groups who is struggling.

Your student:

Profile

How would you support him or her?

A SUMMARY OF **KEY POINTS**

Students with SpLD/Dyslexia often show talent in other areas. It will be your role to ensure that their difficulties do not bar them from succeeding in your subject. There are common challenges across the curriculum which suggest that you should:

> **reduce or compensate for the demands on literacy;**

> **make all tasks, technical schema and expectations clear;**

> **provide structures and scaffold or model the process of developing written work;**

> **provide appropriate vocabulary;**

> **make your teaching as multi-sensory as you can;**

> **give vulnerable learners the opportunity to show and share their knowledge;**

> **avoid copying notes from the board wherever possible (provide notes if essential);**

> **reward positive behaviour.**

Individual subjects pose special challenges. The first step towards inclusive practice is to identify them. You can then ensure that your teaching provides successful ways to meet them. **Remember good teaching for vulnerable students is good teaching for all.**

MOVING *ON* > > > > > > MOVING *ON* > > > > > > MOVING *ON*

This chapter has explored how dyslexia-friendly activities can be applied to the main curriculum subjects. You should consider what is particularly relevant to your day-to-day classroom activities.

Identify two concepts, ideas, suggestions from this chapter that are already part of your current teaching ASK (attributes, skills, knowledge).

Select one new suggestion from the chapter and review and reflect on its implications for teaching in your curriculum area.

FURTHER READING FURTHER READING **FURTHER READING** FURTHER READING

Mortimore, T (2008) *Dyslexia and learning style: A practitioner's handbook*. 2nd edition. Chichester: Wiley.

Reid, G (2005) *Dyslexia and inclusion*. London: David Fulton.

For students with EAL

Peer, L and Reid, G (eds) (2000) *Multilingualism, literacy and dyslexia.* London: David Fulton.

Peer, L and Reid, G (eds) (2001) *Dyslexia – Successful inclusion in the secondary school*. London: David Fulton.

7
Working with number and mathematics

Chapter objectives

By the end of this chapter you should:

- **understand why dyslexia can affect the development of numeracy skills;**
- **understand the definition of dyscalculia;**
- **understand the definition of dyspraxia;**
- **have reflected on dyslexia and dyscalculia and their comorbidity with dyslexia;**
- **as a mathematics specialist, have reviewed your support for all students with SpLD in your lessons.**

This chapter addresses the following Professional Standards for QTS and Core:

Q10, Q12, Q17, Q23, Q26, C31, C35, C37a

Introduction

This chapter looks at mathematics and numeracy in relation to the dyslexic learner. It is divided into two sections. The first section seeks to develop your understanding of the dyslexic learner in relation to numeracy. It defines the difference between dyslexia and the less well understood SpLDs of dyscalculia and dyspraxia. Section two looks in more detail at the dyslexic learner within the mathematics curriculum and how you, as the subject specialist, can dismantle barriers to learning. Throughout this chapter it is important to remember that, although the underlying cognitive differences of dyslexia may present difficulties, many dyslexic learners excel at mathematics due to compensatory learning strengths.

There is no other subject quite like mathematics for dividing us into two emotional camps. Our immediate response is either to say we are good at maths or bad at maths, we like maths or we hate it. Additionally, it appears far more socially acceptable to admit to this weakness than it does to admit to difficulties with literacy. Chapter 6 explored the development of the teaching and learning environment for the dyslexic learner across the curriculum. It gave you the opportunity to explore the barriers to learning for the dyslexic learner in your own subject area and the strategies you could employ in removing these barriers.

Mathematics and dyslexia in the classroom

Mathematics activity pervades the whole curriculum.

PRACTICAL TASK PRACTICAL TASK **PRACTICAL TASK** PRACTICAL TASK **PRACTICAL TASK**

Highlight all the activities below that learners must use in your classroom.

1. Use addition without a calculator
2. Use subtraction without a calculator
3. Use their times tables mentally

4. Use times tables knowledge to divide

5. Use a calculator

6. Use units of length

7. Use units of weight

8. Use units of volume

9. Use units of time

10. Read timetables

11. Estimate

12. Understand and use money

13. Read from a variety of different scales

14. Read from a variety of different charts and graphs

15. Understand temperature

16. Understand negative numbers

17. Use ratio

18. Use percentages, fractions and decimals

19. Use mathematic symbols

20. Use mathematical language

21. Use simple formulas

22. Use 2D and 3D shapes

23. Understand and use angles

24. Add any of your own not covered

After completing the activity above you will see that competency in mathematical ability, in particular numerical ability, is as crucial to the curriculum as that of literacy. Look again at the pattern of dyslexic difficulties presented in the practical task in Chapter 2 and think again about your task analysis. How might these difficulties affect mathematical skills? Chapter 1 explained that definitions of dyslexia develop over time in response to emerging research and practice. Look again at the Dyslexia Action definition of dyslexia from Chapter 1 (repeated below), and the current definition of dyslexia from the British Dyslexia Association.

PRACTICAL TASK PRACTICAL TASK **PRACTICAL TASK** PRACTICAL TASK **PRACTICAL TASK**

Highlight the cognitive features of dyslexia that may cause difficulties with numerical skills to arise for the dyslexic learner?

> Dyslexia is a specific learning difficulty that mainly affects reading and spelling. Dyslexia is characterised by difficulties in processing word-sounds and by weaknesses in short-term verbal memory; its effects may be seen in spoken language as well as written language. The current evidence suggests that these difficulties arise from inefficiencies in language-processing areas in the left hemisphere of the brain which, in turn, appear to be linked to genetic differences.

> Dyslexia is life-long, but its effects can be minimised by targeted literacy intervention, technological support and adaptations to ways of working and learning. Dyslexia is not related to intelligence, race or social background. Dyslexia varies in severity and often occurs alongside other specific learning difficulties, such as Dyspraxia or Attention Deficit Disorder, resulting in variation in the degree and nature of individuals' strengths and weaknesses.

> Dyslexia Action (Formerly Dyslexia Institute) 25.07.2007

Dyslexia is a specific learning difficulty which mainly affects the development of literacy and language related skills. It is likely to be present at birth and to be lifelong in its effects. It is characterized by difficulties with phonological processing, rapid naming, working memory, processing speed and the automatic development of skills that may not match up to an individual's other cognitive abilities. It tends to be resistant to conventional teaching methods but its effects can be mitigated by appropriate specific intervention, including the application of assistive technology and supportive counselling.

British Dyslexia Association October 2007

Can you see now the aspects of the dyslexic profile that might prevent easy development of mathematical skills? Difficulties with language and memory can be crucial.

Spoken language difficulties

Many learners with dyslexia will appear to exhibit no difficulties with mathematical skills. However, there are likely to be underlying language difficulties which may cause some problems. Mathematics has its own symbolic language and students with dyslexia will need to make links between their verbal language and these symbolic representations. This presents the dyslexic learner with two barriers. Activity two will make one of these very clear:

PRACTICAL TASK PRACTICAL TASK **PRACTICAL TASK** PRACTICAL TASK **PRACTICAL TASK**

We use a variety of words to express different operations. Place each one in the correct box. **add, split, sum of, decrease, partition, sum of, increase, group, multiply, and, take away, of, lots of, share, give, minus, times, difference, product of, less than, multiplication, more than.**

+	−
×	÷

You will see from this the huge variety of words used to express one symbol. The second barrier is the fact that we may use the same word to represent different meanings, often subject specific ('equal to' has a very different interpretation in numeracy than it does in citizenship lessons; 'take away' is not the same in a mathematics class as it is in the high street).

What can you do in the mathematics curriculum to support these language skills?

Make explicit the link between the **language** you use and the numeric **skill** required. For example, measure could mean use a: set of scales, protractor, jug, measuring cylinder, stop watch, ruler, string or a time-line. Write the words on the whiteboard and the symbol as you say them. Many students think 'more than' is 'more then'. Do not assume learners know the common vocabulary of mathematics. The following should help to develop this.

- Keep one page at the back of their exercise books for the four basic symbols, and encourage them to add words they do not know as they use them. Colour-code these to aid their memory.
- Build up a class glossary of mathematical terms and their subject specific meaning.
- Keep a simple mathematics dictionary in the classroom that is in alphabetic order. Model good independent strategies – look the word up for the whole class. Do not use a dictionary that separates the four basic areas of numeracy into sections: algebra, number, shape and space and data handling. Students will not necessarily be able to make the link and find the word.
- If you have wifi or internet access in your classroom keep Google images open to link a word quickly with a visual image. (It takes seconds to do this but for many dyslexic learners this helps to establish the 'schema' discussed in Chapter 6 quickly.)
- Use every opportunity to relate the etymology of words into groups e.g. cent, century, centurion, centenary, triangle, triplets, tripod.

Memory

Both the Dyslexia Action definition and the British Dyslexia Association definition include problems associated with memory. To help you in the classroom it is useful to think in terms of short-term memory and long-term memory.

Short-term and working memory

Short-term memory relates to material that must be held in the learner's mind over a period of several seconds. Working memory relates to material that is held in the short-term memory **and** in addition must be integrated and/or reorganised with further incoming information or with information that one has previously learned, sometimes referred to as the 'desktop' of the brain (Thomson, 2004). Learners with dyslexia have smaller working memory capacities than non-dyslexic learners (Pickering, 2004). This smaller capacity causes a variety of difficulties, particularly with all mental arithmetic tasks and mathematical calculations that require a sequence of steps. In addition, working memory difficulties cause problems in sequencing tasks. Working memory and processing speed deficits combine to cause many dyslexic learners to have negative experiences of mathematics, particularly mental arithmetic, and many find the mental arithmetic component of tests at Key Stage 2 and Key Stage 3 national tests daunting. They may panic at any request for mental calculations having had previous humiliating experiences. Working memory weaknesses mean that any request or interruption from a teacher, TA or peer will lead them to forget what they were immediately doing. They may then be accused of either not concentrating on their work or not listening, or both. Memory is crucial to mathematics which builds systematically upon memorised principles, but memory difficulties can cause a range of demoralising incidents across a range of subjects.

- Whilst counting out money they may forget the total amount while focusing on the pound coins.
- In science, whilst using a stop watch, they may forget what observational behaviour they were looking for whilst focussing on measuring the time.
- When counting in French they may have forgotten what number they were up to in English whilst recalling a particular word in French.
- In D&T they may have forgotten the measurement they require whilst adjusting the machinery.
- In dance they may not be able to remember the sequence as well as concentrate on dancing in rhythm.

- In geography the complexities of using four and then six figure co-ordinates rely on good working memory and sequencing skills.

How can you help to support short-term and working memory skills in maths?

There are some basic ground rules.

- Never put a dyslexic learner on the spot and request he works out a mental calculation in front of the class, however simple you think it might be.
- Do not discourage the use of fingers when learners are calculating. In America concrete tools are called 'manipulatives' e.g. counters., number rods, etc. The use of these manipulatives represents a particular stage in the development of mathematical thinking. Learners in the primary stage are currently discouraged from using these in the latter stages of Key Stage 2. However, some learners with working memory difficulties need these manipulatives and are not ready to move on to a less concrete way of operating. If manipulatives are removed, learners will use the one manipulative they have, their fingers. This essential concrete activity is frequently derided as babyish and learners will be embarrassed into concealing it by hiding finger calculations under the table (the decimal system of 10s did not evolve by accident).
- Provide as many manipulatives within your classroom as possible, ensure they are age appropriate (not babyish). Coins, dice, glass beads are all good tools. Have fun, build up a bank of topic specific manipulatives. Do not reinvent the wheel, ask colleagues what they already have in the department, in other departments, in the learning support department. Take your time, you cannot do everything at once as a new teacher.

Overall, make your activities as multi-sensory as you can to encourage the type of deep processing that supports the development of strong traces in the memory. See Clausen May's suggestions for multi-sensory mathematics teaching at the end of this chapter.

Long-term memory

Long-term memory weaknesses mean that the retention of common mathematically-related facts is poor. This creates a vicious cycle – weak working memory difficulties contribute to poor retention of long-term facts. This poor retention of long-term facts then contributes to working memory difficulties, since learners have to calculate over and over again simple facts that other learners have at their finger tips, thus further overburdening their working memory. Being constantly told that they ought to know these basic facts and should learn them demonstrates a lack of knowledge and understanding of why they do not know them in the first instance. Does anyone really think that a learner **chooses** not to learn their times tables, despite the countless opportunities and pressure to do so in primary school? Think carefully before you express surprise at a lack of what you consider to be common knowledge.

Learners may not know many of the following.

- The months of the year in order so cannot relate 1/**10**/2008 to being the first of October.
- Number of days in a year, months in a year, etc.
- Common number bonds.
- How many seconds are in a minute, minutes in an hour, etc.
- How to tell the time. (Being able to read the time on a digital watch does not mean they can relate this

to the 12 or 24 hour clock.)
- The times tables; instead they will go through the process of halving or doubling and adding on which in turn requires large amounts of working memory.
- Common percentages, decimals and fractions automatically e.g. 50%= ½ = 0.5

How can you help learners to compensate for their problems with retaining information in their long-term memory?

The BDA definition of dyslexia above stresses the value of 'supportive counselling'. Competent learners feel intimidated by mathematics. Be consistently understanding and supportive and use the memory skills techniques in Chapter 8 to remember important facts and dates related to numeracy. For example the 21st Century Science GCSE syllabus requires that students know the relative size of micro-organisms in order. '**F**ungus the **B**ogeyman has a **V**omiting **Virus**' puts fungi, bacteria and virus in the correct relative size order and uses the key words.

A number of simple practical measures can reduce tension.

- Always write the date on the board in numbers and figures, e.g. 1st October 2008 (1/10/2008).
- Allow calculators in every lesson.
- Model how to estimate so that learners who rely on calculators can see when an answer 'makes sense'.
- Write metacognitve questions on the board to support independent skills, e.g. break down the learning steps required in order to read the volume on measuring jugs with different scale markings.

Consistently ensure overlearning and reinforcement. In particular, make use of team work across departments. In the primary school, it is very easy to gain an overview of what skills across curriculum boundaries are being introduced and then revisited to provide opportunities for overlearning. Chapter 9 discusses the importance of team work in supporting vulnerable learners. This, however, becomes less easy to implement informally in the secondary school and the need therefore arises for more formal ways of getting together to make inter-departmental links. Schemes of work can therefore be used to make clear who is doing what and at what stage in each term. Once this is mapped per term and per year, it is very easy to see which department and teacher is going to be the first to introduce a skill and who can then reinforce it. For example, which department is the first to **revisit** co-ordinates in Key Stage 3, is it the geography department or the mathematics department? Or does the MFL department introduce 'asking and speaking for directions' in practical French?

Dyscalculia and dyspraxia

Throughout this book you will have noticed that dyslexia is often prefaced with SpLD. It is useful to spend a short time within this chapter looking at some other SpLDs and their definitions and reflecting on the behavioural characteristics that overlap to clarify your understanding. Do not worry about remembering these in depth.

REFLECTIVE TASK

Familiarise yourself with the definitions and behavioral signs of dyscalculia and dyspraxia. What are the similarities to and what are the differences from dyslexia?

Dyscalculia

Dyscalculia is a condition that affects the ability to acquire arithmetical skills. Learners with dyscalculia may have difficulty understanding simple number concepts, lack an intuitive grasp of numbers and have problems learning number facts and procedures. Even if they produce a correct answer or use a correct method, they may do so mechanically and without confidence.

(DfES, 2001)

The behavioural signs of dyscalculia include:

- Counting: dyscalculic children can usually learn the sequence of counting words, but may have difficulty navigating back and forth, especially in twos and threes.
- Calculations: dyscalculic children find learning and recalling number facts difficult. They often lack confidence even when they produce the correct answer. They also fail to use rules and procedures to build on known facts. For example, they may know that 5+3=8, but not realise that, therefore, 3+5=8 or that 5+4=9.
- Numbers with zeros: dyscalculic children may find it difficult to grasp that the words ten, hundred and thousand have the same relationship to each other as the numerals 10, 100 and 1000.
- Measures: dyscalculic children often have difficulty with operations such as handling money or telling the time. They may also have problems with concepts such as speed (miles per hour) or temperature.
- Direction/orientation: dyscalculic children may have difficulty understanding spatial orientation (including left and right) causing difficulties in following directions or with map reading.

(www.bdadyslexia.org)

Learners with dyslexia frequently fail to master the **number** aspect of mathematics due to their difficulties with language, memory, sequencing and processing speed. Despite this, some dyslexic learners are quick to grasp mathematical concepts and, if helped to compensate for these early difficulties, master higher mathematics at university level, although they frequently continue to find number work difficult. There is, however, a subset of learners who do not have language difficulties but display the characteristics shown above. Brian Butterworth (1999, 2004) suggests that these learners do not display a basic competence with numbers that he terms 'numerosity' and terms this smaller group dyscalculic (2004).

Dyspraxia, sometimes referred to as Developmental Co-ordination disorder

The Government website, www.teachernet.gov.uk states:

Learners with dyspraxia are affected by an impairment or immaturity of the organisation of movement, often appearing clumsy. Gross and fine motor skills are hard to learn and difficult to retain and generalise. Pupils may have poor balance and co-ordination and may be hesitant in many actions (running, skipping, hopping, holding a pencil, doing jigsaws, etc.). Their articulation may also be immature and their language late to develop. They may also have poor awareness of body position and poor social skills.

The behavioural signs of dyspraxia include the following.

- Poor gross motor co-ordination skills – tendency to fall, trip, knock things over.
- Poor fine motor co-ordination skills – difficulty with writing, typing, drawing.

- Poor eye tracking skills – difficulty keeping their place when reading a book.
- Verbal dyspraxia giving rise to language difficulties – difficulty pronouncing some words, leading to spelling and writing difficulties and an unwillingness to read aloud.
- Poor sequencing skills – written work appears disorganised.
- Poor short-term memory skills and working memory giving rise to mathematics, reading and writing difficulties.
- Perceptual difficulties – may be oversensitive to sounds, light, touch, smell.
- Self-esteem, motivational difficulties as the result of undiagnosed, or misdiagnosed difficulties and supportive counselling.

As you can see, some of the behavioural characteristics present in the same way with dyslexia, dyspraxia and dyscalculia, but their neurological origin as described by their definitions is different.

In Chapter 3 you learned that there would be learners in your classroom who exhibited behavioural characteristics of dyslexia, but had not been identified or labelled as 'dyslexic'. (This is discussed further in Chapter 9 when looking at the graduated response to SEN as part of the Code of Practice, 2001.) This is perhaps even more the case with dyspraxia and dyscalculia and there are good reasons for this. Research into dyslexia has a long history. This has enabled the development of reliable assessment tools. In addition there are a wide range of recognised accredited training courses for teachers to develop their understanding of dyslexia. More SENCos can now assess for dyslexia and provide in-school training to other members of the school teaching team, thus raising awareness. In contrast, there is to date no reliable assessment for dyscalculia and very little research on the subject. The first screening tool, Butterworth's Dyscalculia Screener, has only been available since 2003. There are more reliable assessment tools for dyspraxia, but training with these in schools is limited and identification is generally made through the occupational therapy service.

Assessing students' specific learning difficulties is a complex task; behaviours change over time in response to life's experiences and our understanding of SpLD deepens. A learner may have more than one Specific Learning Difficulty, in varying degrees of severity and you may be the first adult to recognise the nature of their difficulty. Here are some points to reflect on.

- A learner may have one SpLD.
- A learner may have a range of SpLDs, in varying degrees of severity.
- Very few learners will have a formal diagnosis for their SpLD, particularly dyspraxia or dyscalculia. There are very few learners who have been screened for dyscalculia, but estimates of its prevalence are between 3% and 10% of the population (Butterworth, 2003).
- The Code of Practice (2001) states that provision must be made for all a learner's learning disabilities, not just the predominant one.
- 40% of learners with dyslexia experience some degree of difficulty with mathematics.
- The learner in your class exhibiting co-ordination difficulties may have dyspraxia and/or dyslexia.
- Just as a learner with dyslexia may achieve a higher degree in history requiring high levels of literacy a dyscalculic learner may achieve a higher degree in subjects where numeracy is required.

Finally do not forget that supportive counselling is as important as provision to the learner with SpLDs. Follow the advice in these chapters and you will have the tools to offer this.

Mathematics and the specialist mathematics teacher

As with every subject teacher, it is important for you to examine the specific demands posed by your subject. Chapter 6 explained that learning in any context or subject involves three interlinked stages.

- Getting the information in – modes of presentation.
- Processing the information – storing and revising.
- Getting the information out – modes of expression.

Getting the information in

In many secondary schools mathematics is one of the few subjects where learners are likely to be placed in ability sets straight away, based on their Key Stage 2 results. This poses particular opportunities and barriers for the dyslexic learner. You may have learners who languish in the bottom set for English who are in your top mathematics set. This does wonders for their self-esteem and they act as good role models to their peers in demonstrating that dyslexic learners have a profile of strengths and weaknesses. However, they may still have weak literacy skills, and will certainly be hampered by a less effective working memory. In addition, it is unlikely that a learner in a top mathematics set will have access to a TA, for literacy support. How do you accommodate this in your lessons? How do you introduce a new topic? Do you rely on the text book for learners to read the explanations and examples? Do you insist on silence whilst learners are working through practice questions? Do you allow learners to choose where they sit? A dyslexic learner is less likely to ask a peer for help with reading a question in the text book if not seated next to a trusted friend. Do you use small whiteboards for learners and give them time to try out examples when you introduce a topic, or is the answer given by the fastest thinker? It is likely that you think very carefully about this with all of your learners in lower sets, but tend to forget to take these things into consideration for your more able mathematicians with dyslexia.

Processing the information

Chapter 6 introduced you to the notion of individual learning style preferences (Riding and Rayner, 1998; Mortimore, 2008). The National Numeracy strategy (DfES, 1998) recognises these preferred learning styles and encourages learners to trial a variety of methods. Sometimes, the different way that students respond to tackling mathematics skills can be referred to as 'inchworms' and 'grasshoppers' (Chinn and Ashcroft, 1998). Inchworms like to do things step by step in a logical sequence. They respond well to the rules of mathematics but find it difficult to picture or visualise the mathemtics problem. They prefer to use the following manipulatives: number lines, counting blocks, unifix cubes, white boards, pen and paper. They will automatically show their working out for a problem in tests and exams. Grasshoppers on the other hand can instantly Gestalt the whole problem. (Gestalt is a German word defined by psychologists in 1912 that does not translate into one English word but means 'whole and complete form'.) They are likely to be able to leap straight to the answer intuitively. They prefer to work things out in their head but will use the following manipulatives: Dienes blocks, Cuisenaire rods, graphs, grids and charts. Often, if you ask them how they came to their answer they will have difficulty breaking it down into the sequenced steps. They tend not to show their working out. To be a grasshopper within the exam system you need to be an accurate grasshopper. The exam system, where marks are given for method and ability to show your working, favours inchworms. Many students are flexible in their learning and thinking style. They can be adaptable for the task in hand. Mathematics is one of the subjects where learners experience the most clashes between their own and their teacher's preferred style of learning. Do you think you are a grasshopper or an inchworm? It will influence the way in which you present mathematical information.

Mathematics is a subject where once you as the teacher are sure the initial introduction is understood, learners are able to work through examples in text books or worksheets on their own in order to process and store the information. Do make sure that you do not allow 'differentiation by speed' to operate in your classroom. If learners have slow or poor reading ability, weaknesses in working memory, poor retention of common facts in the long-term memory and slow processing speed, then they will have less opportunity to work through the practice exercises. In addition homework will take longer. How do you accommodate this?

PRACTICAL TASK PRACTICAL TASK PRACTICAL TASK PRACTICAL TASK PRACTICAL TASK

Select a topic from the numeracy strand of Key Stage 3 mathematics.

How would you introduce this topic?

How many ways could this topic be taught?

What manipulatives do you have?

Look in the text book. Do you need a high level of literacy to access the explanation?

Look at the exercises. How could you differentiate the amount/choice of questions, to accommodate the dyslexic learner?

How do you set homework to ensure it is equitable in time, but provides sufficient practice to allow the dyslexic learner to process the information?

Retrieving the information and getting the information out

All learners have learning strengths and weaknesses within the four mathematics strands. Due to working memory deficits, learners with dyslexia are more likely to have learning strengths in shape space and data handling and learning weaknesses in number and algebra. However, the spiralling nature of the mathematics curriculum means that previous knowledge as well as skills must to be retrieved from the long term memory. What can you do to help?

- Use starter sessions to practice a question from the previous topic.
- Set up a 'rolling topics' homework programme. Always set at least one exercise question from a previous topic as well as questions from the topic being worked on.
- Use memory strategies to link language to mathematics facts. The learner with dyslexia may muddle words such as *pentagon* and *hexagon*, and yet be perfectly capable of working out the formula for interior and exterior angles of different regular polygons. You could:
  1. Google an image of the Pentagon;
  2. make verbal links – the number six has an 'x' , the word hexagon has an 'x';
  3. make etymological links as noted in the first section of this chapter with the prefix 'tri'.
- Play games in the starter session, such as 'Guess the topic'. Show a question on the whiteboard from an exam paper, ask learners to tell you which topic it is from by highlighting the key trigger words and justifying their answer.

- Collect a glossary of key trigger words at the beginning of each new topic in their exercise books. Use it as the introduction to the topic when it is revisited at a higher level.

As explored in Chapter 6, students can also be helped to focus on the essential in mathematics problems and to cope better in stressful situations like exams.

- At the beginning of the year liaise with the SENCo to find out any examination or national tests entitlements your learner may have. The learner may be allowed additional time, a reader for exams, or a read aloud facility. Make sure they have opportunities to practise these additional exam skills in ALL tests, internal and external.
- Teach learners how to look for relevant and irrelevant information in wordy mathematics problems. For example, skip proper nouns (names of towns and people) when reading. Some learners will spend ages trying to decode an unfamiliar name in an exam paper. Help students to try out the BUG technique from Chapter 6.
- Point out visual links, for example if an algebra question does not have an equals sign it cannot be worked out, only simplified or factored.
- Allow times table squares at all times. Some dyslexic learners may need to produce their own times table square in the non-calculator exam. With practice this can be reproduced in 3 minutes, and can be used for facts on multiplication, division, factors, squares, square roots and prime numbers (by their absence apart from in the 1 times table).
- For long sequences, such as those required in simultaneous equations, encourage students to make cards with question prompts so that they can think metacognitively when they get lost in the process.

Individual subjects pose special challenges which operate at all three stages of the learning process. The first step towards inclusive practice is to identify the challenges. As with literacy skills, numeracy skills have an impact across all subjects and it is every teacher's responsibility to provide safe learning opportunities to enhance numeric skills. This chapter has not attempted to provide many specific mathematical strategies. Kay and Yeo (2003), Chinn (2004) and Clausen-May (2005) offer full guidance. It simply aims to develop your understanding of how the differences that are associated with SpLD/dyslexia, particularly in terms of memory and language processing, can exacerbate difficulties with mathematics and to suggest ways in which you can adjust your approach to prevent further failure in students who are already likely to be low in confidence.

A SUMMARY OF **KEY POINTS**

> **A triad of SpLDs – dyslexia, dyspraxia and dyscalculia – have been examined.**

> **The common challenges of working memory deficits and the effect that these have on retention and use of long-term memory of mathematical facts have been discussed.**

> **You can ensure that your teaching provides successful ways to meet these demands.**

> **Remember good teaching for vulnerable students is good teaching for all.**

MOVING *ON* > > > > > > MOVING *ON* > > > > > > MOVING *ON*

This chapter has explored how dyslexia-friendly activities can be applied to mathematics across the curriculum and as a specialist subject. You should consider what is particularly relevant to your day-to-day classroom activities.

Identify two concepts, ideas, suggestions from this chapter that are already part of your current teaching ASK (attributes, skills knowledge).

Select one new suggestion from the chapter and review and reflect on its implications for teaching in your curriculum area.

FURTHER READING FURTHER READING FURTHER READING FURTHER READING

Chinn, S (2004) *The trouble with maths. A practical guide to helping learners with numeracy difficulties*. Abingdon: Routledge.

Chinn, S and Ashcroft, R (2006) *Mathematics for dyslexics: A teaching handbook*, 2nd edition. London: Whurr Publishers.

Clausen-May, T (2005) *Teaching maths to pupils with different learning styles*. London: Paul Chapman Publishing.

DfES (2001) *Guidance to support pupils with dyslexia and dyscalculia*. London: National Numercay Strategy.

Henderson A (1998) *Maths for the dyslexic: A practical guide*. 2nd edition. London: David Fulton.

Kay, J and Yeo, D, (2003) *Dyslexia and maths*. London: David Fulton.

Robson, P (2001) *Maths dictionary*. 2nd edition. Scarborough: Newby Books.

Yeo, D (2003) *Dyslexia, dyspraxia and mathematics*. London: Whurr Publishers.

8
Study skills

Chapter objectives

By the end of this chapter you should:

- **understand study skills in relation to personal development;**
- **understand study skills in relation to subject content, including revision skills;**
- **know about IT skills support;**
- **understand the skills required for examinations including special exam arrangements.**

This chapter addresses the following Professional Standards for QTS and Core:

Q17, Q23, C35

Introduction

In this chapter we will aim to answer the question 'What are *Study Skills*?' *Study Skills* is an umbrella term, used to encompass a variety of techniques, skills and thinking methods. Some individuals are fortunate enough to absorb these easily. They develop the ability for effective study naturally as their education progresses. However, many students with dyslexia do not develop study skills naturally and need to be taught them and given opportunities to practise and trial different study skill methods in safe learning environments before they encounter important key milestones in their education. More importantly, students with dyslexia need to recognise the transferability of study skills, both between topics within a subject area, and between subject areas.

This chapter seeks to provide you with an overview of the types of skills required and, where appropriate, to encourage you to think about the theoretical relationship between these skills and the characteristics of dyslexia. The key aim is to support you in teaching and to highlight the transferability of these skills within your subject.

Dyslexia 'looks different' behaviourally in differing age groups. Chapter 2 discussed these behavioural differences in detail. For example a very young child with dyslexia may be struggling to repeat nursery rhymes, a ten year-old child may still be having difficulty learning to read, whilst an adult will have mastered the skill of reading but may still be having problems remembering the content of what she has just read. Similarly, different study skills will be needed at differing stages of a person's development and education. However, becoming responsible for and monitoring one's own learning is an essential part of a person's development. Therefore introducing study skills as a concept should form an integral part of your teaching support within the secondary curriculum.

Study skills in relation to personal development

This practical task is designed to help you reflect on the ways in which difficulties with personal development impinge upon your lessons and whether you are offering solutions to these barriers or exacerbating difficulties.

PRACTICAL TASK PRACTICAL TASK **PRACTICAL TASK** PRACTICAL TASK **PRACTICAL TASK**

Select a specific class that you teach.

What lesson do they have before yours? Why is it important to know this?

Do they use exercise books or folders to record their learning? What advantages and disadvantages do these different methods offer? Discuss your responses with a colleague.

What equipment should they bring to your lesson?

What support framework do you offer to students who do not bring equipment? Is it based on punishment or reward? Why is this important for you, and for your students with dyslexia?

When, and how, in the lesson do your students record what the homework is in their planners?

At what stage in the lesson do you collect written homework?

Organisational skills and effective time management

Young children take very little responsibility for organising themselves. However, as we get older, there is an increased need to take on this responsibility. Whilst definitions of dyslexia focus upon phonological deficits and dyslexia as a language based disorder, (Chapter 1) there is general agreement that many students with dyslexia have poor organisation skills. These manifest themselves in several ways, including difficulty organising time, difficulty organising the necessary materials required for a specific purpose through to difficulties organising extended pieces of written work.

Students with dyslexia often lack temporal awareness (a sense of themselves in space and time). Although many may master the skill of **telling** the time using a digital watch, students may not have the same ability to '**feel** and manage time'. This can cause several problems. A Year 7 student told to 'Finish what they are writing in the next ten minutes' is likely to stop writing straight away or to feel that they have plenty of time to complete their work. A GCSE student faced with several coursework deadlines from different subjects is likely to leave homework that was set that day, but which is not due in until next week, only to find they have forgotten what they have to do when they come to complete the task. Students working at Diploma and A level are liable to mismanage work with extended deadlines and leave it until the last minute, only to find that they have left too much work to complete and their 'just in time' management skills have metamorphosed into 'not enough time' skills.

It is often difficult for those of us without dyslexia to see such problems as genuine disabilities. Parents and teachers will often accuse such students of being lazy or unfocussed and expect them to try harder. Whilst it is important to improve such skills, their absence all adds to the stress of the student with dyslexia.

So how can you, as the teacher, intervene to support time skills?

To help them gain a 'sense' of time:

- Ensure the students have a feel for blocks of time. Link ten minutes to an activity that they enjoy which takes that amount of time.
- Use a popular and invigorating piece of music that lasts about two minutes. Play this at the beginning, or end of a lesson whilst they get out or clear away equipment within the time deadline.
- When setting timed tasks, use a timer to show them the amount of time passing. Tell them when five minutes has passed. Encourage them to spend longer periods of time engaged in one task.
- Ensure that, if they read the time with a digital watch, they also understand time.

To help them to plan and manage their time:

- Encourage students to write the date in full on their work (days of the week, the month and the year) to encourage over-learning of such skills. (These are life skills and not to know them is embarrassing. Many students with dyslexia could not instantly tell you that the 28/7/08 is in the month of July.)
- Support them in using their homework organiser or planner. Use highlighter pens to note the day work is due in, write it in the due as well as the date it was set. In this way they will begin to see if a specific day is starting to get overloaded. Some school timetables ask for homework to be handed in on days when they do not have the subject. Alternatively, teachers ask for books and folders in on days when the students do not have their subject on the timetable. This often means students carry every book in their bag at all times to be safe.
- Encourage the use of 'timed and signed' strategies when setting homework. If homework is set for 30 minutes ask students to only complete 30 minutes and have their parent or carer (or themselves by Key Stage 4 and above) to sign either the work or their diary to say this has been completed. Otherwise how do you as the teacher know how much they can manage independently in the time set? How can you be equitable in the amount of homework you set?
- In older students encourage the use of a time manager, either an electronic or paper based one, whichever suits. Encourage them to write down all their appointments, both social and work related.
- Although not study related, ensure they place in their diary important birthdays, when the clocks change in the autumn and the spring, term start and finish dates, etc. Continually forgetting important dates or arriving late for appointments all adds to the picture of themselves they present to the outside world as a disorganised person and affects their self-esteem.
- Support them in planning extended pieces of work. Start with the date the work is due in and work **backwards** in the diary, putting in deadlines for the final write up, handing in the draft, research period, etc. By breaking the work up like this and working backwards they will be able to see the latest date at which they can start each small part of their work.
- Teach them to **prioritise** work in the time available. Every teacher quite naturally is dedicated to their own subject, but be aware that students may not have prioritised your subject as a high priority towards the end of Year 9 or Year 11.

To help them prepare for the timed exam:

- Ensure that if students have additional time for external examinations that they have an opportunity to practise how to use this in all course work and end of unit tests, as required in England in the guidelines issued by the Joint Council for General Qualifications (2008). Special exam arrangements will be returned to later in Chapter 9.

Becoming an effective learner

What makes an effective learner and what types of knowledge might help you to support your students with dyslexia? Howard Gardner (1983), himself at one time a failed student forced to repeat a year of schooling, introduced the concept of multiple intelligences. Broadly these intelligences are: analytical intelligence, pattern intelligence, musical intelligence, physical intelligence, practical intelligence, intra-personal intelligence and inter-personal intelligence. One can see that different cultures may value the differing intelligences to a greater or lesser degree. Which intelligences are valued within the education system? Which intelligences do we as a society currently pay large sums of money in admiration of?

Whatever your feelings as regards the validity of the idea of multiple intelligences, the importance of each one, or the hierarchy you would place them in, there is no doubt that people need intra-personal intelligence in order to study successfully. Intra-personal intelligence deals with a person's own ability to self-monitor, self-motivate and set targets. Some students find these skills easy, but the majority of students do not. They will need you to help set small targets for them and to celebrate when such targets have been reached. Higher level intra- personal skills will involve students in analysing feedback from their assignments in a metacognitive way so as to learn from their experience, as discussed in Chapter 5. What did I do that helped this essay to be successful? How can I repeat and transfer these skills the next time I require them? If my essay comment states that my work lacked detail how can I find out what next step I need to take in order to move towards a more detailed response?

Study skills in relation to content

Note taking

The barriers to learning that difficulties with reading and writing present for students with dyslexia, and the ways in which as a teacher you can overcome some of these barriers and support the development of literacy skills are dealt with in Chapter 5. However, it was noted in Chapter 6 that students with dyslexia struggle with note-taking skills. Such skills are crucial in all subjects; for thinking skills, coursework, extended essay writing, research and revision, and will be dealt with in detail here. We will look at several methods of note taking below. There are two important points to bear in mind when reading, and using these.

1. Not every method will suit every learner in your class. Chapter 6 discussed learning styles and the fact that you should never make general assumptions that all students with dyslexia have similar preferences. For example, mind mapping is a useful way of making notes, but it does not suit everyone. If you always provide frameworks of mind maps as the note-taking method in your classroom you are creating barriers for some learners. Teach a variety of note-taking techniques (remember that due to your own preferred learning style, some of the methods you teach will not suit your way of working). Offer students an open choice of note-taking methods as part of their learning.
2. Encourage students with dyslexia to be metacognitve about note-taking techniques. What methods do I know that would suit this piece of work? What methods have I used before that work for me? In order to do this students need a safe learning environment in which to trial their methods. (Learning a new technique to use for a piece of assessed coursework is probably not a good idea.) You need to give opportunities for

note-taking skills to be trialled in class work and homework. When you set note-taking tasks, ask students to comment on the note-taking technique they used, why they chose it, and whether they think it was effective. Teach note-taking skills from Year 7 onwards when the content is smaller and they can focus on the skill of note taking.

Methods of note taking

Using the 6 Ws

This is a simple, easily transferred skill that develops metacognitive skills. Students can either take notes using each of the 6 w words; **who, what, where, when, why, how** in a linear way or in a spider gram. Spider grams work well for making notes from information such as videos, which can jump about in presentation of facts. As the teacher you can offer frames for the 6 ws to begin with. Suggesting questions within the **why** section that they need to find out, or giving clues as to the number of people contained in the **who** section, will provide a scaffold.

Using skimming skills for note taking

Skimming skills have been mentioned briefly in Chapter 5. Skimming skills allow the reader to get the gist of the content. Dense pages of reading can be reduced to good notes using advanced skimming skills. In turn, using this note-taking skill enhances reading skills. Skimming should be an active, not passive, process. Here is the process:

Highlight the title. Add one fact you already know about the title. (For students with dyslexia this ensures that they are primed with the correct schema to help them to predict and process the likely language and upon which to hang their new information.)

Highlight the subheadings. Count them. If there are three subheadings there are three sub-topics to make notes on.

Count the paragraphs within each subtopic of the text. If there are six paragraphs within the text then there are six pieces of information within the subtopic. Students often know this skill when they write. But, they often fail to **transfer** this knowledge to other authors' writing as part of their note-taking skills.

Highlight the first sentence in each paragraph. This is usually the key sentence.

Highlight the key word within the key sentence or, if there is a key phrase, condense its meaning into one key word. Is this paragraph part of what they need for the notes you have asked for? Is it relevant? Have I already made notes on this topic? They may not need to read it.

Highlight the last sentence in each paragraph. This makes sure they have not missed a key point from the previous paragraph or the paragraph from which they are taking notes.

Group note taking for videos, internet research, etc.

It can be useful to ask groups within the class to focus on one topic or section of the note taking. This encourages students to look for **relevant** and **irrelevant** information in relation to the task. This is a vital note-taking skill. When watching videos you can use the alphabet to aid note taking. Divide the class into four groups, and give each group responsibility for a quartile of the alphabet letters (e.g. A–E, F–M, n–S, S onwards). As students watch the video, they note key ideas that start with any of the letters of the alphabet they have responsibility for. (The notes can be a drawing or a key word which does not have to be spelled correctly.) After the video, the group collates group notes, the group notes are then collated into class notes. The teacher models organising the notes collected with the whole class. Remember, however, that some dyslexic students will struggle with the letters of the alphabet so be aware of this potential pitfall.

Time lines These are useful for information that needs to be sequenced e.g. chronological reports and notes for science investigations. Students with dyslexia have difficulties sequencing information. You can provide frames in the early stages of learning this skill. Chapter 6 provides some ideas and there is a model in Appendix 3.

Fortune lines Similar to time lines, fortune lines allow students to plot events in a sequence against successes and failures of people and characters. They are useful for note taking in: history, RE, character studies in English literature, history of music or art. Ensure that if students have additional time for external examinations that they have an opportunity to practise how to use this in all coursework and end of unit tests, as required in England in the guidelines issued by the Joint Council for General Qualifications (2008). Special exam arrangements will be returned to later in Chapter 9.

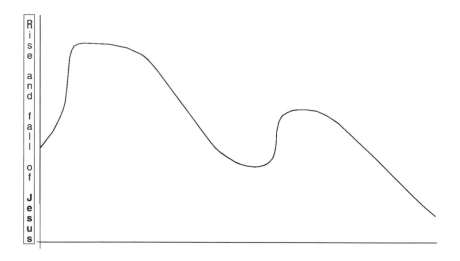

Figure 8.1 Events e.g. Fortune line of Jesus from Palm Sunday to the Crucifixion

Mind mapping©

Mind mapping© is a useful way of taking notes by reducing text to key words and adding pictures, colour and symbols. It is an active skill that needs to be taught and modelled if it is to be used for note taking. It is best taught as a revision skill and then transferred to note taking once the skill of mind mapping has been mastered. Read books, such as those by Tony Buzan (e.g. 1982). Look on the internet and learn to mind map, use assistive technologies such as mind mapping software, discussed towards the end of this chapter, so that you can show your students this skill in a multi-sensory way. You can provide frameworks of mind maps in the early stages, but mind mapping is creative and personal and therefore pre-published mind maps are only of use to students in the early stages of learning this skill.

Picture and key word method

This is a useful method for students who like, and are good at, drawing. Students draw a line down the page vertically. They make picture notes of the important points on the left hand side of the page. They can either add key word notes at that point, or wait until group work when key ideas and notes can be shared. This form of note taking also allows them to correct and add details that they may have misinterpreted as a result of reading difficulties (Dupree, 2005).

A last word

To be effective notes need to be used **after time has elapsed** from the original information gathering. If you ask students to make notes, do give them opportunities to return to the notes and see if the notes were detailed enough to be of value.

PRACTICAL TASK PRACTICAL TASK **PRACTICAL TASK** PRACTICAL TASK **PRACTICAL TASK**

Select a text from your own subject area. Using as many of the methods above as suitable make notes. Then, using a search engine, find another article on the same subject.

Study skills in relation to content: revision and memory skills

To be successful within the education system, students have to demonstrate knowledge, understanding and skills. Inevitably this will take the form of end of Module or Course exams. Exams require good memory skills. Memory deficits will therefore have a significant impact on these skills, and in particular on knowledge based skills. As noted in Chapter 6, there are three main difficulties for students related to memory: 'putting it into the store', 'keeping it in the store' and 'getting it out of the store'. Whilst psychologists hold pessimistic views as to the effectiveness of any programmes claiming to improve cognitive memory deficits (Turner, 1997), there are several skills and techniques that students can be taught in order to make the most efficient use of the memory capacity that they have.

Processing the information

As a teacher, the subject specific language that you use every day can subconsciously become part of your own general lexicon of language. If you shadow a Year 7 class throughout one school day, you will be amazed at the amount of new language that is introduced. The majority of people store new vocabulary using phonological codes, but students with weak phonological awareness will make use of alternative, semantic codes (Snowling, 1987). Therefore, to be effective leaners, students need to be given hooks and links so that the new vocabulary is stored in an appropriate place for easy retrieval. An essential component of revision is to be able to store the key words required in an organised way.

You can help the storage of new vocabulary in several ways.

- When using key word lists, always ensure students have a list of key subject specific words that they understand. Link the new words to words they are already familiar with. For example, the word *basin* in geography needs to be linked to possibly: *flood, delta, river*. Always choose a link that is already familiar. Don't turn the exercise into a spelling one.
- Create visual images and families to help storage: for example the Triangle Family, QUEEN ISOCELES, tall and slim, KING EQUALATERAL, fat and plump, PRINCESS RIGHT ANGLE, lazy and propped up against the wall. Their ALIEN DOG called SCALENE who can change shape.

● Link visual images to the meaning of words. For example drawing clock faces in the letter Os in the word chronology, drawing the word *'basin'* in a basin with water flowing from the tap into it.

Keeping it in the store

It is a sad fact that you will forget 80% of this chapter within 24 hours of having read it (Buzan 1982). This is the same for everyone. It is essential to review information in order to keep it active within your memory. When many students come to revise for an exam, they find that they have forgotten everything they were originally taught and are having to relearn the entire syllabus again. **Reviewing** your learning is an essential study skill, particularly during revision periods in the lead up to exams. When planning the revision timetable students need to build in **reviews** so that their timetable is a spiralling one.

CASE STUDY

Alex has been taught how to complete simultaneous equations. Every time he tries to do them again, he has forgotten the process. It is a difficult one for a learner with dyslexia – it has a long sequence which affects working memory skills and also requires the retrieval of long-term facts, using tables. Alex has been shouted at by his teacher for having forgotten how to do them. In a study skills session in the learning support department, Alex discusses this problem. The learning support teacher goes through the steps to find out where in the process Alex forgets. The teacher then writes a set of metacognitive questions on a prompt card for Alex, that he can ask himself as reminder prompts within the process. Alex uses the questions as prompts and uses the text book to practise one simultaneous equation each day for a week. By the end of the week he is no longer having to read his prompt card, he has internalised the metacognitive questions. He reviews one question each week in the learning support department, and by the end of 6 weeks feels confident that he can leave them for a month and review once later before the exams.

During a study period you are more likely to remember what you covered at both the beginning and the end of the session and forget the middle portion. This means that you must ensure that study periods are not too long, otherwise the middle chunk becomes large and more is forgotten. You may be surprised to know that length of concentration span is linked to how old you are, 1 minute of concentration for every year of your age. (How often do you talk 'at' students for longer than 10 minutes?) Study periods for individual topics should be about 20 to 25 minutes in length maximum.

Retrieving the information

There are several techniques, or tools for supporting students' memories and retrieving information.

Mind mapping[©] Devised by Tony Buzan, mind mapping is a way of maximising linkage between ideas using visual and verbal cues. It does not suit everyone. Some revision guide-books now publish mind maps as well as linear notes. However, mind maps are personal, and need to be made actively by the students themselves. If they are made at the end of each unit of work, and you use starter sessions in your lessons as opportunities to review them, they are very useful for end of course exams, but they are time consuming to produce.

Word association using the number peg system This is excellent when information has to be remembered in a sequence, but can also be used to remember key headings for essays in exams. It relies on both visualisation techniques and rhyme. Some students, with very poor phonology therefore find it useless, as they cannot remember which item rhymes with which number. Examples of how to use the number peg system can be found in Dupree (2005) or Mortimore (2008).

Telling a story An alternative method to the number peg system is to make up a sequenced story. For example relating a story of the journey of a sandwich through the digestive system ensuring the nutrients and enzymes are linked in memorable ways.

Mnemonics Mnemonics can be useful and are the most commonly used and known memorising tool. However, many students with dyslexia, with word storage difficulties, do not find this method successful; they can remember the mnemonic but forget what word each item is associated with. Try to make the mnemonic meaningful to the subject matter.

As a teacher you need to be aware of as many as possible; some will suit you, and your dyslexic students more than others. Again, opportunities for trying out the various techniques need to happen in a safe learning environment and when the end result of the assessment is not too important.

IT resources for study skills

Overview

The depth and breadth of IT (Information Technology) or ICT (Information and Communications Technology) available for students with dyslexia advances daily. The purpose of this chapter therefore is to encourage you to embrace the idea of technology as effective support tools for students with dyslexia for study, even if you find your students' knowledge on these matters is far in advance of your own. Do ensure that students are not made to feel they are 'cheating' by using IT tools. They are tools which help to prevent barriers being placed in the way of learning.

PRACTICAL TASK PRACTICAL TASK **PRACTICAL TASK** PRACTICAL TASK **PRACTICAL TASK**

Make a list of all of the IT tools you use or have used recently to support your own study. Once you have the list see if you can group the tools into categories.

Students with dyslexia benefit from the IT resources and categories listed below. However, whether they have access to these will depend on several factors.

- The level of difficulty their dyslexia creates as a barrier to learning.
- Their Code of Practice placement, School Action/Plus, Statement of SEN, which is then linked to their entitlement to resources.
- The financial situation of their parents – many students with dyslexia will rely on parents to buy large pieces of equipment such as laptops, and software such as voice activated software, which is expensive and requires an up to date computer to run it successfully along with training in its use.
- The personality and learning style of the dyslexic individual – whether they are an IT native or an IT

Immigrant (which most people over the age of 30 are).
- and finally **YOU**, that is whether you make it clear that, in your eyes, the use of a range of IT tools is a way of working 'smarter' not 'harder' of creating differentiation and breaking down barriers to learning. This will mean that the students in your care will feel they can use them legitimately to demonstrate their learning and to support their study skills.

What categories of ICT use did you come up with in the previous activity? Here are some of the most common:

- **Organising time and work**
  Utilise PDAs such as Blackberry personal organisers, mobile phone, Microsoft Outlook. Whilst mobile phones are excellent resources for helping to organise the student with dyslexia they are banned from many schools. Many schools now have their own websites, which have important key dates, etc. Find out how the school website is used in your school.
- **Finding out information**
  Make use of a range of internet sites. Do not dismiss YouTube as a social site, it has a vast resource of useful film clips for all subjects, There is a wealth of useful revision sites, general research sites and teacher resources sites. However, you might like to consider how 'dyslexia-friendly' these sites are in their content and presentation styles and how technology might enable your students to access them more effectively.
- **Reading and understanding**
  Voice-activated software, scanners and scanner pens, Text to speech programmes such as Via Voice Gold, highlighter facilities on Word programmes. All of these can unlock text for learners and these programmes can be used to access websites too.
- **Organising information**
  Search the internet for free downloadable mind mapping software to help organise writing. Inspiration is used and appreciated by many dyslexic students. Encourage students to use PDAs for organising themselves.
- **Writing and making notes**
  Again, use the mind mapping software. Some dyslexic writers' lives are transformed by the voice activated speech to text software such as **Dragon Dictate**, Naturally Speaking or by recording devices and word prediction software.
- **Learning, remembering, revising and doing exams**
  Chase up the internet sites. Encourage students to make and share PowerPoints of information that they are trying to remember or understand. Use the mind mapping software to create revision concept maps, embellished with pictures, and test their knowledge independently or with a study partner. In this way you can save them from being dependent on ancient and scrappy notes and on the written word.

As fast as we recommend a programme or site, it changes and develops. Hence we have provided few web addresses. It is strongly recommended, however, that you view the website www.dyslexic.com. This is a website that specialises in IT resources for students with dyslexia of all ages and it reviews materials and assesses the extent to which they are 'dyslexia-friendly'.

Finally, there are always free downloadable resources to support students' study skills. These are constantly changing.

http://www.iespell.com This is a free spell checker which allows students to store their personal word lists. It can be used in several applications, including MSN, etc. This is a really useful tool for students with dyslexia.

http://freemind.sourceforge.net/wiki/index.php/Main_Page This is free mind mapping software. There are others, that allow free trials but this software allows free use.

http://sense-lang.org/typing/ This is a free touch typing programme for those students who cannot afford, or who do not like to use voice activated software and need to learn faster touch typing skills.

http://www.microlinkpc.co.uk/downloads.php For students with dyslexia this company have an excellent piece of free software called 'Colour Explorer'. It allows students to change the colour of the screen word colour, word font, etc. in several applications. Yet at the click of the mouse the computer will restore to the normal default settings.

http//www.readplease.com This allows you to download a free text to speech reader.

There are many other free software downloads available, and they do change all of the time. As an NQT, ensure you share those that you have found and feel are useful with your colleagues. Most of all use them, and share them with your students.

Access arrangements for external examinations

Access arrangements are additional arrangements put in place for students by your school, prior to their taking external examinations. The aim of these arrangements is to ensure that candidates have a fair opportunity to demonstrate their learning. They should not be confused with the special examination arrangements that are granted **after** a student has taken an exam because, despite appropriate preparation for the exam, sudden 'adverse circumstances beyond their control' (e.g. the sudden death of a close relative, car accident) has affected their performance.

The Joint Council for Qualifications (JCQ) is responsible for overseeing the policy and fair use of these access arrangements and they are reviewed each year. There are many types of access arrangements. The profile of strengths and weaknesses displayed by students with dyslexia will determine his or her eligibility for arrangements selected from this list.

- A reader.
- A scribe.
- Read aloud facility (a room where they can read aloud without disturbing others).
- Coloured overlays.
- Examination on coloured paper.
- Transcript (if their handwriting is difficult to decipher).
- Voice activated computer.
- Word processor.
- Additional time.

The JCQ have strict criteria for the allocation of these facilities. Some arrangements can be determined by the school, others must be approved by the examination's awarding body or board. It is usually the responsibility of the examinations officer and the school SENCo to organise and decide upon access arrangements, therefore, you do not need to concern yourself with this aspect. However, access arrangements should cover the entire course and so should be applied for as early as possible. They should also be part of a normal student's working arrangements and this means that you have a responsibility to give these students every opportunity to practise using the facilities awarded. It is pointless having 25% extra time and a reader for external exams in Year 11, if at no point during Key Stage 4 has anyone given you the opportunity to learn how to use the additional time, how to dictate your answers or how to settle to work answering exam questions with a reader by your side. Make sure you are aware of which students in your class are eligible for access arrangements and that you try your utmost to accommodate them as part of your normal classroom teaching and to help them make these strategies part of their normal study and assessment practice.

A SUMMARY OF **KEY POINTS**

This chapter has explored how students, with SpLD/dyslexia-friendly activities can be encouraged to develop organisational and study skills to help them across the curriculum. You should consider what is particularly relevant to your day-to-day classroom activities.

MOVING *ON* > > > > > > MOVING *ON* > > > > > > MOVING *ON*

Identify two concepts, ideas, suggestions from this chapter that are already part of your current teaching ASK (attributes, skills knowledge).

Select one new suggestion from the chapter and review and reflect on its implications for teaching in your curriculum area.

You might like to consider developing your own knowledge of study skills by finding out about courses such as the online study skills courses offered at http//www.brainwaveseducationcourses.com

FURTHER READING FURTHER READING **FURTHER READING** FURTHER READING

Basic Skills Agency Catalogue: Commonwealth House, 1–19 New Oxford Street, London WC1A 1NU Tel. 020 7405 4017

Beard, J (1994) *Basic study skills.* Stafford: Crossbow Publications.

Dupree, J (2005) *Help students improve their study skills*. London: David Fulton.

Lewis, M, Wray, D (1996) *Writing frames; scaffolding children's non fiction writing*. University of Reading: Language Information Centre.

Mortimore, T (2008) *Dyslexia and learning style. A practitioner's handbook.* 2nd Edition. Chichester: Wiley.

Townend, J and Turner, M (2000) *Dyslexia In practice: A guide for teachers*. New York: Kluwer Academic/Plenum Publishers.

PART 3
SPREADING THE LOAD

9
Working as a team

Chapter objectives

By the end of this chapter you should:

- **understand the roles and responsibilities of team members: teacher, SENCo, teaching assistant, Senior Management team, LA specialist support team, other outside agencies, parents/carers, peers and the student;**
- **understand the graduated response of School Action, School Action Plus and the Statementing Process in providing for a student's special educational needs as part of the SEN Code of Practice (2001), together with your role and responsibilities;**
- **have reflected on the management of teaching assistants and the impact of working with teaching assistants in your own classroom;**
- **understand the function of Individual Education Plans, Group Education Plans and your role in providing and monitoring their effectiveness;**
- **have reflected on best practice in making parents/carers of students with dyslexia feel included as team members.**

This chapter addresses the following Professional Standards for QTS and Core:

Q3, Q11, Q14, Q20, Q24, Q26, Q32, C14, C21, C31, C40, C41

Introduction

Teaching can on occasions be a profession where you can feel isolated. There are very few other working roles where one adult spends the majority of their working day in the company of children and separated from adults. But importantly, teaching is a profession in which team work is vital. There are many different teams that form in schools. As a newly qualified teacher, you will need to seek the guidance of more experienced members of teams that you are part of. As part of your training when in schools you will have become a temporary team member of faculties, worked across curriculum teams, with your Heads of Departments in your subject area and attended whole school meetings run by members of the senior management team on whole school issues. This chapter aims to explain some of the roles and responsibilities of team members in relation to supporting your teaching of students with dyslexia. As such, you need to know your place in the team in relation to the Code of Practice for Special Educational Needs (DfES, 2001). Your place in this team may be less familiar to you.

Understanding the roles and responsibilities of team members

The move from primary school to 'big school' is an important one for every student. However, for the student with special educational needs this transition period is even more important. Students with dyslexia move from the classroom where only one teacher, one teaching assistant and the SENCo need to know how to prevent the barriers to learning which might arise from their learning strengths and weaknesses, to a position where they need several teachers to understand their requirements. In turn, each teacher sees the student for less time each week and so it takes longer to build up a personal picture of the particular learner's needs. As this team becomes larger, the importance of formal record keeping and shared information and goals takes on more importance.

The role of the Special Educational Needs Co-ordinator

The role of the SENCo in secondary schools is a central one, and due to their responsibilities many SENCos are also part of the senior management team. The time required in most secondary schools to fulfil this role ensures that this is a full time position. This is not the case in many primary schools where the SENCo may also be the Head Teacher or have a full time teaching position in addition to their SENCo role. The Code of Practice for SEN (2001) notes the following as roles for the SENCo in the secondary sector.

> *Overseeing the day to day operation of the school's SEN policy*
> *Liaising with and advising fellow teachers*
> *Managing the SEN team of teachers and learning support assistants*
> *Coordinating provision of pupils with special educational needs*
> *Overseeing the records on all pupils with special educational needs*
> *Liaising with parents of pupils with special educational needs*
> *Contributing to the in-service training of staff*
> *Liaising with external agencies*

(Code of Practice, 2001, p65)

The role of SENCo is not one that is usually filled by an NQT, and so logically you will note that SENCos in secondary schools have had previous teaching roles and have additional subject expertise in at least one curriculum area. This means that they have experienced the demands of whole class teaching and record keeping. Good SENCos will use this knowledge to ensure that the expectations of you as a class teacher, in ensuring the SEN policy is delivered are reasonable. Alongside their experience, there is a wide range of additional qualifications that a SENCo may have. However, you cannot expect them to be an expert in every aspect of SEN provision, and not all SENCos will have a post-graduate qualification in the theory, assessment and teaching of students with dyslexia. Whilst there may be another member of the SEN team with such a qualification, we are still a long way off from every secondary school employing at least one teacher with this qualification.

What will the SENCo expect from you as part of the team?

1. The SENCo will expect you to follow the school's SEN policy. In addition you will be expected to follow all other school policies; such as marking policies, handwriting polices and homework policies. Many problems brought to a SENCo's attention by parents/carers can be avoided if school policies are adhered to. For example, if you set homework to be completed on a night not allocated to it in the homework diary, you may overload students and their parents/carers. As part of the role the SENCo will be the point of contact for any aggrieved or upset parent of a child with SEN who wishes to log a complaint, and it is then the SENCo's responsibility to liaise with the class teacher or teachers who caused the difficulty.
2. The SENCo will expect you to know which students in your class are on the school's special needs register, and the stage of the Code of Practice they have reached.
3. They will expect you to deliver some of the provision for those children with SEN, as written within their Individual Education Plans (IEPs). As the Code of Practice Notes *All teachers are teachers of pupils with special educational needs* (p59). For those students with a Statement of Special Educational Need, the provision, as written in their individual statements, is a legal right. If it is noted that a student should have 'alternative means of recording their learning', you will be part of the team that ensures this legal right happens in your lessons. We will return to statements later in this chapter as part of understanding the graduated response to SEN.
4. They will expect you to contribute to the setting of targets for IEPs and the recording of when these are achieved, so that, as SENCo, they can oversee this record keeping effectively. In many primary schools it is the class teacher who writes the IEPs for students at early stages of the graduated response.
5. They may ask your permission to withdraw a child from some of your lessons in order to deliver other parts of the student's provision. There is no ideal lesson from which to withdraw students, but for some students with dyslexia this one to one or small group teaching is essential. Negotiate times practically, and be sympathetic to students returning to the classroom who may have missed elements of the lesson or curriculum content due to additional provision being delivered in the learning support department.

What will the SENCo do for you?

1. Give you an up to date copy of the school's SEN policy. (This must be reviewed annually by the governors of all secondary schools.)
2. Give you a list of the students you teach who are on the school's SEN register.
3. Share with you all IEPs. We noted above that the SENCo's responsibility is to oversee provision. It is your responsibility to deliver this and, to do this effectively, you will need to know what targets are on a student's IEP. IEPs should only record *that which is* additional to *or* different from, *the differentiated provision which is in place as provision for all pupils* (p70). So, to say that you always differentiate all lessons anyway is not sufficient. You must help deliver the actual targets written in the students' IEPs.
4. You can expect the SENCo to support you in developing your understanding of the wide ranging SENs of the students in your class and to provide you with advice and training. This may include supporting you in managing the teaching assistants working in your class.
5. Chapter 3 noted that you may approach the SENCo if you suspect a student in your

class should be on the SEN register and is not. Check your school's SEN policy for how the identification of students is managed.

The Local Authority specialist support team

This is a team of specialist advisory teachers. Each team member specialises in a different area: hearing or visual impairment, specific learning difficulties including dyspraxia and dyslexia, communication disorders such as autistic spectrum disorder, speech and language difficulties and so on. Their role is to support the SENCo and spend time teaching individual students in school, particularly in transition to Year 7. They are responsible for providing LA training to teachers and teaching assistants. As part of their role, they may observe students in your lessons. They will offer staff advice at all stages of the graduated response to special educational needs, This is particularly so if a student is placed on School Action Plus or is being assessed for a Statement of Special Educational Need, where evidence gathering is required. They will also attend annual reviews of statements. Whilst you will not often come into contact with the specialist team, they are there if you wish to seek advice. You should do this through your SENCo.

Teaching assistants

TAs play a key part in the SEN team and their numbers in school have increased dramatically over the past five years. However they are not automatically as great an asset as they might seem. Well-trained, sensitive TAs with whom you have established a good rapport are worth their weight in gold (Margerison, 1997). They will have built good relationships with students in the group and will offer a wealth of experience and suggestions as to how you can work together to support individuals. You will tactfully need to establish the nature of your TA's role and background knowledge. Some TAs are assigned to specific students as part of the learner's statement provision. Other TAs in your classroom may have a more general support role for a number of students within one class, particularly if your school sets students by ability. Talk to the SENCo who should be able to help you establish their role in your classes. You will then need to discuss with the TA what role he or she has played previously to get a picture of his or her understanding. A poorly trained or badly managed TA can set up barriers between the supported learner and the rest of the class and stigmatise the learners he/she is meant to be helping (Ainscow, 2000).

A sensitive well-deployed TA can be seen as an asset and a source of support by all students in the class while keeping an eye on the specific students who will need the help. All the ground rules for teachers in creating a dyslexia-friendly class apply to TAs as well. You may like to talk together about his/her understanding of the implications of SpLD and to check that he/she is comfortable with the ground rules for teachers. It is essential that your adherence to these principles is not undermined by other adults in the classroom as this will give mixed messages to the rest of the class which will not necessarily encourage them to be supportive. Ensure TAs you work with follow the ground rules.

Ground rules

- Encourage students' strengths.
- Do not expose their weaknesses.
- Provide opportunities for success (however small) and then praise it. However, beware of hollow praise – your students will see straight through this.

- Ensure that they are aware of the progress they are making.
- Encourage all students to think and talk about the ways in which they learn and then allow them to use their preferences and strengths whenever possible.
- Encourage them also to explain their difficulties to the teacher, TA or supportive peer/s so that you can co-operate to find the best ways to support them to develop independent strategies.
- Try to establish a fairly steady routine to create security and ensure that all students have taken in any instructions you may have given.
- Be prepared to explain many times in many ways but do not publicise a student's failure to understand.
- Don't expect a dyslexic student to be able to do two things at once (e.g. write and absorb instructions simultaneously).
- **Never** forget how embarrassing failure is.

Additional ground rules when working with TAs in your classroom

- Share the aims and objectives of each lesson with the TA.
- Discuss with TAs when they can talk with students and when you require silence. There is nothing more disruptive to your lesson than insisting on silence whilst you give out instructions, only to hear the TA talking. Decide between you when they can repeat/clarify points in the lesson and provide opportunities for talking.
- Do not always leave the TA to work with the targeted students. This can create a barrier between you and the student; you understand the students' strengths and weaknesses less, making it more difficult for you to provide appropriate learning experiences.
- Discuss the reward system in your class and how the TA will be involved with this, e.g. giving out stickers and awarding merits. This needs to be managed consistently.
- Be aware a TA may arrive late to your lesson for a very good reason. They have to move around the school between lessons and sort out and return lost homework organisers!
- Remember the SENCo is responsible for managing TAs. If you are having difficulty, discuss this with your SENCo.
- Do not let the TA do everything for a student. This will not create independent learners.

The teacher

From reading both the SENCo and TA roles, you can see that the teacher's place in the team is central to the successful provision of all students with SEN. *All teaching and non-teaching staff should be involved in the development of the school's SEN policy and be fully aware of the school's procedures for identifying assessing and making provision for pupils with SEN* (Code of Practice, 2001, p15). Most student teachers and NQTs realise their responsibility here and this is emphasised by the Code of Practice. However, you may still find some 'dinosaurs' in your school who would prefer to abdicate this responsibility.

Parents/carers

CASE STUDY

Mr and Mrs Stevens have three boys at Rickdon school. All three boys have dyslexia, as does Mr. Stevens. One of the boys has severe dyslexia and has a place in the school's specialist dyslexia unit. The other two boys have mild dyslexia, but Mr and Mrs Stevens chose the school for them too, since it has developed a dyslexia-friendly ethos. Mrs Stevens is the only person in the family with good organisational skills and both parents work. In one afternoon's food technology lesson the students will be making coleslaw. Mr and Mrs Stevens have forgotten to buy the ingredients for their son in the morning and Mr Stevens arrives at the school reception at lunch time and asks to see his son's form teacher. She arrives and he asks if they can talk somewhere quietly. He explains to her that he left the ingredients list at home and has bought what he thinks is right, but is not sure. The form tutor looks in the bag, and sees carrots, mayonnaise and a lettuce rather than white cabbage. She has a good relationship with Mr Stevens and explains that he has remembered to buy a round light coloured vegetable, but the wrong one! She tells Mr Stevens not to worry, she will sort it out. He smiles at his mistake and goes off happily. The form tutor finds Mr Stevens's son and asks him who his study buddy is. (The SENCo uses a study buddy system for all students with SEN – someone who is a friend with strengths in areas where their buddy has weaknesses.) The study buddy has a whole white cabbage and is happy to share it. The form tutor halves the cabbage during the lunch hour. Mr Stevens's son arrives in class with the correct ingredients in his own bag.

Chapter 4 has already discussed parents/carers as part of the team and given some practical advice on homework and its impact on the family. For many students with dyslexia, difficulty with organisational and memory skills can make the links between home and school less strong. In primary school, parents/carers may have relied on conversations with other parents or carers at the school gate to keep them up to date with day-to-day school planning, school trips, dates for school fetes and non-uniform days. This is unlikely to be possible at the secondary school. The case history here seems such a small, trivial matter but highlights team work. Mr Stevens felt able to approach the school receptionist with his request. He felt able to approach the form tutor, who was happy to see Mr Stevens in her lunch hour straight away. His relationship with her was such that he did not feel embarrassed to ask for her support and, knowing the family background, the form teacher knew to take action herself. Such action strengthens the bond between home and school so that on the occasion when things run less smoothly (and there will always be such occasions, however much planning you do) parents/carers are less likely to feel aggrieved.

Making parents/carers feel valued members of the team occurs at both formal and informal levels. As part of all students' provision, links will be made through the homework organiser, end of term reports, parents' evenings and, in many schools, reward systems which send home letters of praise. In addition students with SEN have formal IEPs, which are sent home termly and shared with parents/carers before being reviewed. Students with a Statement of Special Educational Need have a legal entitlement to an annual review to which parents/carers are invited. If difficulties have been allowed to build up during the year, or suitable provision for their child's needs has not been provided and parents/carers' views have not been valued in solving those difficulties, they will be formally noted at this point.

What can you do to make parents/carers feel valued as team members?

- Recognise parents/carers as experts in understanding their child's strengths and weaknesses.
- Recognise that dyslexia has heritable characteristics; parents may also have literacy, memory and organisational difficulties.
- You will probably be a form tutor, use this role to establish good links with your parents or carers.
- Use the homework diary as a means of communication. Look in it, read any comments from parents/carers and reply to them so they know you are interested.
- If homework diaries need to be signed by parents or carers, make sure you check this each week.
- Recognise their child's strengths as well as weaknesses. Write praise and notes to parents/carers in exercise books and the homework organiser.
- If you give out letters or forms ensure that students write down in their homework organiser 'give mum

or dad letter/form.'

- If you set an end of unit test and parents/carers spend all evening helping students revise for it – then ensure you give the test.
- Don't use parents' evenings to lecture parents/carers. Be as good a listener as speaker.
- Sometimes a phone call is a good way of sorting out delicate issues. It is more personal. Establish a time that is convenient to you both when you can phone. Share the purpose of the call first, so parents/carers have time to think about their response.

Students and peers

Chapter 4 has already discussed the importance of peers in creating a dyslexia-friendly class. The central role that students play as team members is embedded in the Code of Practice. *From an early age children with SEN should be actively involved at an appropriate level in discussion about their IEPs including target setting and review arrangements and should have their views recorded* (Code of Practice, 2001, p34). This emphasises how important the student's voice must be in the whole process. As students move into Key Stage 3 they will take more responsibility for managing their own learning difficulty. They will be involved in setting and reviewing their own targets and, if they have a statement, will probably for the first time be attending their annual reviews. It is important they feel valued members of the team. In Chapter 3 we noted that Mark was the first person consulted before his class teacher took action and spoke to the SENCo.

Other team members

There are other team members that you need to be aware of. Each school must have a school governor responsible for SEN. He or she is responsible for ensuring the SEN policy is delivered, and will often observe lessons. The Connexions service (a public service for offering information and advice for young people) works with all young people between the ages of 13 to 19. Some students will have little involvement with the service, but others may have significant contact with Connexions through their **personal adviser**. Many large schools have personal advisors from the Connexions service based in school and they work closely with SENCos, form tutors and the senior management team.

REFLECTIVE TASK

Now that you have read about the team members and your place in that team, think about how it operates within your current school. Read or re-read the school's SEN policy. What parts of the policy do you see in practice? What aspects of the policy in your school meet the requirements of dyslexia-friendly schools as explored in Chapter 4?

The graduated response to Special Educational Needs

As with many special educational needs, within the Code of Practice, dyslexia exemplifies a continuum of need, ranging from mild to severe. The Code of Practice was first written in 1994 in recognition of the need for a graduated response, and to have accurate records and evidence of students' failure to make adequate progress along this continuum, despite appropriate intervention. There are three stages, school action, school action plus and a Statement of Special Educational Need. First written in 1994 it was updated in 2001 to take account of the Special Educational Needs and Disability Act, 2001. Section 317A of the

Education Act 1996 means that parents/carers must be informed if their child has SEN, and at whatever level of need they are perceived to lie within this graduated response to need.

Within your classroom there will be students with dyslexia, placed at all stages of this graduated response, who:

- have a statement of Special Educational Need;
- are placed on school action plus;
- are placed on school action;
- are not on the school's SEN register.

This graduated response looks hierarchical, but is not intended to be. It is not a race to see if students can be moved up the ladder towards the statement, though in reality parents/carers and SENCos will often feel aggrieved at the lack of resources directed at students who fall below the level of school action plus. The key test of whether a student is placed at the correct stage is if there is evidence that progress is being made within the current provision. Hence a deaf child could enter nursery school with a Statement of Special Needs, whereas a child with dyslexia may take several years before one is issued, as with Jodie in Chapter 3. The assessment of dyslexia and the nature of its commonest behavioural characteristic – a failure to acquire literacy skills – means that there is often a model of 'failure' to read and or write with repeated levels of intervention before a student may reach school action plus or be issued with a statement that provides the appropriate level of provision. But the Code of Practice states clearly that any sign of developing literary difficulties of the sort that hamper progress in some areas of the curriculum should be a trigger for intervention. The appropriate levels of support at school action or school action plus are designed, in many instances, to be proactive and to prevent the need for a Statement. This means that record keeping of provision and progress made is vital if this graduated response is to be effective.

All feeder primary schools inform the secondary school of every child on their SEN register and his or her current level of provision. Key Stage 2 results will provide additional evidence before transition of the appropriate stage. In addition LAs have moderating procedures across schools to ensure that a child placed on school action plus at one school has the same level of difficulty and a similar level of provision as those at other schools. However, do not assume that every child entering secondary school will have been placed on the register and, in practice, there is often wide variation between schools' SEN provision as students make the transition from a primary to secondary school. In addition the students' needs change over time, as we noted with Mark in Chapter 3.

At *school action* students with dyslexia in secondary school will probably have all of their provision delivered within the mainstream class. They may have TA support in some areas of the curriculum and perhaps attend a readers' club or spelling club in tutorial time. LA specialist teachers may have been involved in the information gathering but it is likely that the team consisted of: parents/carers, teachers, SENCo, TAs and child. But without the daily structured reading practice provided in primary school, they may fall further behind.

At *school action plus,* provision for students with dyslexia should involve in-class support and withdrawal tutoring to address their literacy difficulties. They will have more TA support time allocated to them in class. They should be provided with extra time and if necessary a reader for all end of module tests. The effect of this additional support must be recorded.

This helps provide evidence of need when external exams are due, where rigorous criteria must be met to obtain additional special exam arrangements. External agencies, such as the educational psychologist and specialist support team will have been involved in collating evidence of need and suggesting appropriate provision.

Neither school action nor school action plus are statutory requirements. If a student fails to make progress, parents/carers or school can request an Assessment of Special Educational Need. This assessment must be completed within six months, evidence is gathered from a wide range of external agencies and, for those students with severe need, a Statement of Special Educational Need is issued. This is a legally binding document. It has six parts, three of which are important for you to understand; **part 2** sets out the special educational needs of the child, **part 3** sets out the provision including additional resources provided by the LA and **part 4** names the placement i.e. school in which this will be provided. All statements must be reviewed annually to ensure that the needs remain the same and that the provision has a) been delivered and b) should remain the same. At the annual review, all team members discussed above will be invited to attend, including you.

PRACTICAL TASK PRACTICAL TASK **PRACTICAL TASK** PRACTICAL TASK **PRACTICAL TASK**

Ask the SENCo if you can see the Statement of a student with dyslexia. Familiarise yourself with the terms used in part 2. Note that not all LAs use the term *dyslexia*. Some prefer to use specific learning difficulty, some refer to literacy difficulties and phonological difficulties. Look at part 3. Which parts are your responsibility? How would you adapt your lessons to deliver this provision? What advice would you like from the SENCo to help you deliver this?

Individual Education Plans

Whatever stage of the Code of Practice a student is placed on, he or she will be issued with either an Individual Education Plan (IEP) or a Group Education Plan (GEP), often used at school action for groups of students who experience literacy difficulties. In response to the government's personalisation goals, some schools now refer to IEPs as PEPs (Personal Education Plans). IEPs should include information about six things (Code of Practice, 2001, p54).

- The short-term targets (no more than 3 or 4) and increasingly in secondary schools set by the student.
- The teaching strategies to be used.
- The provision to be put in place.
- Success or exit criteria.
- When the plan is to be reviewed.
- The outcomes of the review.

In secondary schools reviews generally take place once per term. Most schools use software packages to generate IEPs. Find out what the IEPs in the school you are working in look like. The quality of IEPs can vary. In some schools they are excellent. In other schools the targets written are too generalised and appear to require no provision on the teacher's part in order to be met, with all the effort and emphasis placed on the home and child. If you are asked to contribute to a student's targets make sure they are SMART in relation to your knowledge of the student's learning strengths and weaknesses, the support you can provide and the progress you and the student would like to see.

The acronym SMART stands for
   Small steps
   Measurable
   Achievable
   Realistic
   Time related

PRACTICAL TASK PRACTICAL TASK **PRACTICAL TASK** PRACTICAL TASK **PRACTICAL TASK**

You have been asked to contribute to a target for Natasha. Natasha is in Year 7 and has a Statement of Educational Need for dyslexia. One target on part 3 of her objective states *Techniques for tackling self-organisation should be incorporated into her IEP*. However there are other students in Natasha's class placed at school action and school action plus for whom this target is appropriate. The SENCo has advised that this could be a target suitable for a Group Education Plan (GEP) in this class. Write a GEP that focusses on this target in relation to a specific curriculum area.

External examinations

You may have students in your class with dyslexia who are eligible for special arrangements for external examinations at Key Stage 3, GCSE, Diploma and A Level. Special arrangements are made for candidates with permanent or long-term disabilities or learning difficulties, such as candidates with visual impairment. Some of these, such as extra time, may be authorised by the school. The arrangements for others, such as a reader or an amanuensis, must be approved by the awarding body before an examination. There are strict criteria for such arrangements, and they differ at Key Stage 3 and Key Stage 4. The types of special arrangements that students with dyslexia are likely to require include: extra time (usually a maximum of 25%), a reader, read aloud facility (a room where they can read out loud rather than in their head without disturbing others), an amanuensis, use of a laptop, rest breaks. Most students who are eligible for special arrangements will be registered at school action plus or have a Statement, but not all. As a class teacher you should complete the following.

- Talk to the SENCo to see who in your class is likely to be eligible.
- Find out who the examinations officer is in your school. All arrangements will go through your examinations officer.
- Ensure that, wherever possible, students have opportunities to practise any of the special arrangements they may ultimately use in external exams. (The special arrangements must be part of a student's normal working procedure and you will need to provide evidence of this in your classroom.)
- Approach the SENCo if you think you have a student in your class not on the school's SEN register who may need special arrangements.

A SUMMARY OF **KEY POINTS**

> **This chapter has summarised your role in the team providing provision for students with SEN, including dyslexia.**

> **It has considered your role within the context of a whole team and the requirements of the Code of Practice, 2001.**

> **It has looked at the graduated approach to providing support for students with SEN and considered special exam arrangements.**

MOVING *ON* > > > **> > >** MOVING *ON* > > **> > >** MOVING *ON*

Ensure that you have read the school's SEN policy and all related whole school policies. Does your classroom reflect good practice? Review the list of students on the school's SEN register and the information for you as class teacher.

FURTHER READING FURTHER READING **FURTHER READING** FURTHER READING

DfEE (2000) *Working with teaching assistants: a good practice guide* (ref: DfES 0148/2000).

DfES (2001) *Special Educational Need Code of Practice* (ref DfES/581/2001).

www.everychildmatters.gov.uk

10
Managing behaviour

Chapter objectives

By the end of this chapter you should:

- **understand the importance of avoiding the creation of situations that give rise to conflict and distress within your classroom;**
- **have explored ways of doing this.**

This chapter addresses the following Professional Standards for QTS and Core:

Q2, Q31, C1, C2, C37a

Introduction

The majority of newly qualified teachers are likely to spend more sleepless nights worrying about how to cope with challenging behaviour than about any other demands the job may make. This chapter will not provide you with lists of behaviour management strategies – effective use of the teaching strategies offered in earlier chapters should help to prevent problems. A small proportion of your students will exhibit profound difficulties with behaving appropriately within the classroom context and a range of practical and academic texts exist to help you with these individuals. However, it is not the case that SpLD/dyslexia usually brings with it any deep rooted primary behaviour difficulties. There is some evidence that it may sometimes be accompanied by attention deficit disorder (ADD or ADHD), or Asperger's syndrome with its range of idiosyncratic behaviours (DePonio, 2004) however, the majority of students with dyslexia whose behaviour is challenging are likely to have acquired these behaviours as a response to their difficulties with learning within the school environment. Once these students are supported appropriately and the damage that failure and insensitive handling have done to their concept of themselves as learners is addressed, these defensive responses tend to disappear.

What are your expectations?

What might you expect from a student with SpLD/dyslexia? At this stage, you need to review the information offered in Part One about the impact of SpLD/dyslexia upon behaviour. Think particularly carefully about how this might make a learner with undiagnosed comorbid SpLDs think about him- or herself, about teachers, schools and learning.

PRACTICAL TASK PRACTICAL TASK **PRACTICAL TASK** PRACTICAL TASK **PRACTICAL TASK**

Think about a skill that you have found particularly difficult to acquire. This might be something as complicated as statistical analysis or as simple as knowing what to say when you find yourself face to face with someone you have fancied for ages. Then think about a time when you had to use this skill, particularly in public, and failed.

If you are someone with no flaws, you might like to try writing five sentences about yourself with the hand you don't usually use. How difficult and slow was that? For some dyslexic students, writing is always like this. Now try with your writing hand and just feel the difference it makes to what you can say.

How do these 'failures' make you feel? Hot with embarrassment, flustered, resentful, angry with the person who put you in this humiliating position. Teachers are frequently people who have experienced very little academic failure throughout their school careers. The humiliation tends to be particularly acute when the skill is something other people seem to find really easy and when the failure is hard to conceal. Sensitivity to learners' feelings is central to working successfully with vulnerable students. How can you avoid adding to a vulnerable student's discomfort?

Supporting strengths and weaknesses

PRACTICAL TASK PRACTICAL TASK **PRACTICAL TASK** PRACTICAL TASK **PRACTICAL TASK**

Think back to Chapter 2 and list in columns 1 and 3 the strengths and weaknesses you might expect to find in a student with SpLD dyslexia.

1. Strengths	2. Your subject	3. Weaknesses	4. Your subject

Look back to Chapter 4, first practical task, chart two. Experience and research (Hales, 2004; Edwards, 1994; Riddick et al., 1996; Scott, 2004; Mortimore and Crozier, 2006) would suggest that, regardless of an individual's profile, the confidence and self-esteem of most students will have been damaged and your first goal is likely to be to win their trust and make them feel that your classroom is not a place where their difficulties will be highlighted or exposed. Much disruptive behaviour is simply a defence – getting in before you do – and will diminish when the level of threat reduces.

Now consider Chapter 6, think of your own subject area and classroom environment and consider which specific areas of weakness might be triggered. Note these in column 4. Consider this as a form of 'risk analysis'. For example, why might a field trip put a dyslexic student under pressure which might lead to confrontation? Examine different aspects of the trip right from the start where the student has to get an information letter/parental permission slip home to the parent and back to school by a particular date to get his name on the list. You may find that this is an area where your teaching assistant can offer support. Ways in which all members of the team – including the student, peers, parents, teachers, teaching assistants and others – can co-operate to help individuals to develop independent strategies were explored in Chapter 9. You may feel that you do not have the time to consider all this and you will be overwhelmed with other demands. However, this type of 'risk assessment' once done, is in place for all trips, will help a number of students within the class and may well prevent unpleasant surprises.

How might the student's strengths be useful? Note these in column 2. Think about how you might use these to improve the learner's image within the class. You should not forget that each student with SpLD/dyslexia will have his or her own profile of strengths and weaknesses along with preferences for ways of working. This activity allows you to consider how you might individualise the way in which you present your subject to allow the student to use his or her strengths and compensate for any weaknesses.

What sort of teachers do students with dyslexia respond to?

Studies (Thomson and Chinn, 2001; Thomson, 2004) asked students and discovered that students were put off by teachers who:

- shout;
- rush;
- show you up;
- give too many instructions.

They stated that their ideal teachers should be:

- clear, concise, pleasant, calm, patient and prepared to repeat information.

They said,

> When I am stuck I know I can put my hand up and not get shouted at for not listening. The teacher smiles at me and then explains it again, doing at least two examples with me.

> Good teachers aren't ignorant and unsociable people. They can notice when you are having problems and they don't dismiss you by ignoring you and your questions.

Thomson (2004, in Reid and Fawcett, 2004, p251)

Thomson and Chinn (2001) built up a wish list from the students they interviewed. Here it is.

Do:
- give help discreetly (and quietly) to individuals;
- give more time;
- offer catch up exercises;
- provide handouts with summaries of work/information/tasks;
- mark work tidily and selectively in dark colours (not blood red) and provide praise and clear, constructive comment;
- judge work for content not spelling;

- give grades that can show individual improvement;
- allow students to work in smaller groups;
- develop your awareness of SpLD;
- care.

Don't
- go too fast – don't rush me;
- wander off the point;
- patronise me;
- demand too much copying or dictating;
- read out test results or display 'league tables';
- be sarcastic or ridicule me;
- tell me off when I'm asking a friend for help;
- confuse being dyslexic with being stupid;
- make me read aloud in class.

Many of these points will have already been made in earlier chapters describing teaching approaches for the dyslexia-friendly classroom. It is important to remember how much your choice of teaching and communication strategies will affect the behaviour and attitude of your students. Much of the challenging behaviour may be a response to your way of dealing with the student and is therefore preventable. Appropriate strategies give rise to co-operation, trust and mutual respect.

These two aspects will be key.

- Building trust and confidence.
- Individualising your approach.

Avoiding conflict

Most people dislike conflict. Students report that they hate teachers who shout (Mackay, 2004) and research shows that stress undermines learning. Your knowledge of the difficulties that accompany dyslexia should help you understand why, how, when and where small conflicts might emerge and grow into big confrontations if handled inappropriately.

CASE STUDY
Ella (13) severe dyslexia
It was on a Monday. It was PE. I'd got my kit but was late for the bus and left it in the kitchen. I knew that Mrs. Johnstone would give me a hard time, probably a detention, but she pulled some horrible smelly stuff out of the lost property box and made me put it on. It was too small for me and bits of me stuck out where they shouldn't. Everyone was laughing and I was so embarrassed. Later on, I got some horrible texts on my phone. I do try to remember things but it's really hard. Next time I'll just bunk off if I haven't got the right stuff. I'm not going through that one again.

How would you handle this? What advice might you provide for Ella, for Mrs Johnstone or Ella's tutor?

(You will probably find it interesting to share this activity with other colleagues and members of your team.)

Examine the main difficulties experienced by a learner with dyslexia (reading; spelling; phonological difficulties; written expression; organisation; memory; automaticity; speed of processing; sequencing).

Look at the following table which illustrates a range of situations that could lead to conflicts and tears and provides some exemplar solutions. What solutions might you have suggested? There is no 'right' solution. Each individual, context and situation is different. Appendix 6 provides you with a blank Conflict Prevention Chart. You might find it useful to consider the difficulties experienced by students in your group, how you might be able to prevent confrontations and compile a chart for yourself. Try to familiarise yourself with the possible systems, provisions and sources of help available in your institution so that your suggestions are practical and realistic.

Table 10.1 Conflict prevention

Type of difficulty	Situation	Problem	People involved student and	Possible solutions
Reading	Maths exam	Unable to read test sheet	Exam invigilator Maths teacher	Special access arrangements made; communicate with exam co-ordinator, SENCo
Spelling	Science project	Range of new terminology to spell	Science teacher Teaching assistant	Provide key words in advance/use adapted IT
Phonological difficulties	Modern Language lessons	Pronouncing new vocabulary	MFL teacher	Encourage the use of multi-sensory methods
Written expression	History homework	After good oral performance, produces scrappy work	New colleague	
Organisation	Drama	Unable to find drama studio or bring appropriate footwear	Drama teacher	
Memory	Arranging a school trip	Bringing paperwork, money, etc.	Tutor Parents Peers	Structure and use homework diary effectively
Automaticity	Homework	Given homework instructions orally at end of lesson while packing up – fails to produce homework	Class teacher	
Speed of processing	Dance	Talented dancer has difficulty with sequences of steps	Dance teacher Peers	
Sequencing	e.g. Alphabetical order	Finding names in research index	Any teacher or peer involved in project research	

A factor present throughout all these situations is the need for **communication** between all involved. Without this knowledge and understanding, it will be hard to develop positive relationships between students, their peers and staff. Communication is not always easy in a large secondary school and it is not always clear as to whose responsibility the creation of links might be. As a class tutor, you might need to think about whether this is part of your role and, if so, how it can be made manageable. Chapter 9 suggested some ways of making teamwork easier but you will need to ensure that you consider your own context and how to do this. You may find that the SENCo already has advice and information available for colleagues but this may not always be widely disseminated. As time passes, you might be able to combine your experience with information provided here to compile an advice sheet to share with colleagues within your department.

Key aspects

The focus throughout this chapter has been upon how building positive relationships can affect classrooms. The importance of mutual trust and respect emerges repeatedly in the literature (e.g. Thomson and Chinn, 2001; Scott, 2004; Mortimore, 2006). Six Cs should characterise these relationships.

They should:

- instil **confidence**;
- be **constructive** rather than confrontational;
- develop **competence** rather than dependence;
- respect the need for **confidentiality**;
- be **consistent**;
- encourage **communication**.

Confidence

It is easy to overlook how demoralised many students with dyslexia have been as a result of experiences throughout their primary education. During adolescence, the peer group tends to reign supreme and students are keen to establish their identity or image with their peers. Many individuals with dyslexia do not see themselves as learners and, to compensate, may aim to make an impression in less constructive ways. You may need to re-establish their confidence to engage with any task by enabling them to experience some success, however seemingly small. You are likely to need to break tasks into small, rewardable steps and initially support the student through these steps. Your teaching assistant may be of help here. Try to avoid a focus upon areas where the students will struggle, such as spelling or accuracy. Scaffold the stages of work without doing the work for them. You are trying to promote a 'can do' attitude. One way of managing difficult behaviour is to attempt to ignore the negative and reward the constructive. This approach is not foolproof but will often work with a student who is seeking attention and does not care what sort it is. Try to discover if the student has skills and talent in other areas and acknowledge them – maybe he is a skater, perhaps she can paint. Seek out positive aspects of the student's work and behaviour to reward, whether verbally or through whatever rewards system you or the school has devised. However, do not patronise these students. Tact is vital.

> ### CASE STUDY
>
> When Gareth was given a prize on his history trip, his first response was 'You haven't given me this because you feel sorry for me, have you?' We hadn't!
>
> Karl (14 and a non-reader from a pupil referral unit) initially found it impossible to accept praise or take personal credit for success and used it as another way to cause trouble and be offensive until he was able to see from quantitative scores on reading tasks that he really was beginning to make small steps of progress.

You will also have to guage how public this praise needs to be. Not all teenagers want to be seen to be pleasing their teacher! If a student has carefully created an antagonistic image, it may be difficult for him or her to 'come around'. However, if the student is aware that you are not going to expose his or her shortcomings and humiliate him, however, unwittingly, he may begin to feel that you are allies in this learning process.

Constructive relationships

If students have been exposed to consistent failure and to criticism from teachers, it will take some time for them to begin to trust you not to be like the others. Building confidence, differentiating and structuring tasks for success, giving genuine praise when it is due, encouraging students to try their hardest and acknowledging the effort that has gone into a piece of work – even if it is not particularly good – these will all build a constructive relationship.

The other side of this is to anticipate and, without abdicating control to the student, to avoid confrontation. You will need to develop sensitivity to the signs that an individual is getting wound up and know when you can deflect and when you do need to confront. If confrontation is inevitable, you need to explain clearly why the situation is as it is. Avoid raising your voice, use the 'broken record' technique of quietly repeating the same request or explanation until the student either understands or gives up. Do not get drawn into the student's argument or get yourself into a corner where there is no honourable way out for either of you. Make it absolutely clear that it is the behaviour, not the student, that is unacceptable and that bygones are bygones once the particular situation is resolved. Never resort to sarcasm – you will frequently find the student either has no idea what you are talking about or else is better at it than you are!

Do not underestimate the power of a negative or positive relationship. Adults with dyslexia recalling their early school experiences remember with startling clarity both those who have caused them pain and those who have supported them effectively (Mortimore, 2006). Teachers who work in a special school environment frequently report how it is only when a dyslexic student has been through his or her repertoire of acquired destructive behaviours and begun to trust the staff, that learning becomes possible (Burden, 2005).

Competence

Establishing a supportive relationship must be one priority. However, your aim throughout is to help the student to develop competence and become an independent learner. There is a danger that students may come to depend on a teacher or support worker to the extent that they develop what is sometimes termed 'learned helplessness' (Seligman, 1990). This is associated with lack of persistence in the face of failure and a passive attitude to learning and to organising their lives. The student may thrive while able to access the support and then fall apart when he or she moves on to Further Education, University or the workplace. It is a constant balancing act between offering appropriate scaffolds and encouraging the student to take responsibility, to cope with failure and to develop the strategies necessary for surviving it.

The key must be to offer students a choice of strategies and to insist that they take responsibility for selecting the ones that suit them. For example, teach her how to utilise a diary or palm top to organise herself and then back off and expect her to use it. If he cannot master the written word to express himself, get him competent in the use of voice recognition software such as Dragon Dictate and help him to decide when and how to use it independently.

Students with dyslexia need at an early stage to start thinking about the ways in which they learn best and how to make the most of the various types of resources available in schools and FE or HE institutions. Students moving into FE will find that, when they come to apply for additional support for their dyslexia, they are suddenly categorised as 'disabled', a stigmatising label which they have never previously applied to themselves, and often the cause of real distress. If you are a personal tutor or involved in careers advice or pastoral support, you will need to encourage the students to reflect objectively about themselves and to identify what they want their future lives to be like and how they might go about achieving their aims regardless of any difficulties posed by their dyslexia.

Confidentiality

A student's trust will enable you to support his or her learning. It takes time to build up but can be destroyed instantly by a tactless remark or revelation. It is up to the student to decide how much of his or her dyslexia should be disclosed to others, whether they be classmates or other staff. In an ideal world, nothing but good would come of making dyslexia public – it would help to inform others, develop understanding and tolerance and go a long way towards making classrooms dyslexia-friendly. However, children report many negative responses to their dyslexia (Humphrey and Mullins, 2002) and it will be up to you to establish with the student what needs to be kept private.

Consistency

Learners with dyslexia are likely to welcome consistency in a range of areas. Many have found school life intensely threatening in its unpredictability and will like a sense of routine, knowing what to expect and where things are. This will be particularly true of any students with Asperger's syndrome who live their lives according to their own personal routines. Some students with dyslexia find it hard to organise themselves and therefore like to know what they are doing and what it will involve in terms of equipment or forward planning. Others, of course, operate in a much more spontaneous way and enjoy the challenge of change and surprise. All these students, however, will welcome consistency in their relationships with you. They are likely to respond to clear boundaries and clear expectations and to need to feel secure that you will not suddenly and unpredictably fall out with them. They are often so used to being on the wrong side of teachers, often without knowing exactly why, that having at least one teacher who seems consistently to relate positively to them will make a real difference to their school lives.

PRACTICAL TASK PRACTICAL TASK PRACTICAL TASK PRACTICAL TASK PRACTICAL TASK

Applying the ideas

You may already have a student, with dyslexic type difficulties, whose behaviour is causing you concern. Use the chart below to identify his or her profile and suggest how you might manage him successfully. If this applies to none of your students, how might you manage the behaviour of the following individual? He seems likely to cause difficulties in the group before long if he is not included in a positive way. It may seem that you use up a lot of your time collecting the information you need and thinking about this individual but it will pay for itself in terms of reduction of future difficulty within your class if you can get him on your side.

> Richard arrived in your classroom halfway through the autumn term of Year 9. He has moved three times in the past four years as the family have moved frequently and recently lived abroad. It is now coming up to Christmas. He has quickly settled into the class but has joined a group of potentially disaffected boys and is beginning to create difficulties to attract their attention. He usually fails to carry out instructions quickly and is frequently off task when independent work is required. When redirected he can be rude and dismissive although he is surprised when reprimanded. He has shown interest in your subject when information is presented via video and can make relevant and creative points, but this does not happen frequently. His written work is brief and badly spelt and homework is seldom completed. This particular class has a small group of boys who are difficult to handle and Richard is sometimes involved in name calling.

What information would you attempt to collect?
Who would you consult?
What would you do?

A SUMMARY OF **KEY POINTS**

The six Cs:

> **Communication;**

> **Confidence;**

> **Constructive relationships;**

> **Competence;**

> **Confidentiality;**

> **Consistent behaviour;**

will go a long way towards managing behaviour and preventing confrontation and unhappiness. If you combine these with a clear knowledge of the impact of the strengths and weaknesses associated with dyslexia and use of the teaching and learning strategies provided in this book, many difficult situations and challenging behaviours should be prevented and your classroom should be a happier place. You should also find that many of these approaches are equally useful for other learners, both vulnerable and resilient. They will not always work, but the number of uncomfortable incidents should be reduced.

MOVING *ON* > > > > > > MOVING *ON* > > > > > > MOVING *ON*

The following practical task now considers how you might support other staff who are likely to encounter these learners.

PRACTICAL TASK PRACTICAL TASK **PRACTICAL TASK** PRACTICAL TASK **PRACTICAL TASK**

Supporting other staff

Look back over this chapter and Chapter 2 and compile a list of dos and don'ts that might help other staff to manage the behaviour of any learners with dyslexia in their classrooms.

FURTHER READING FURTHER READING **FURTHER READING** FURTHER READING

Burden, B (2005) *Dyslexia and self-concept*. London: Whurr Publishers.

Long, R (2007) *The Rob Long omnibus edition of better behaviour*. London: David Fulton/NASEN.

Mortimore, T (2008) *Dyslexia and learning style. A practitioner's handbook.* 2nd Edition. Chichester: Wiley.

11
The dyslexia-friendly school

Chapter objectives

By the end of this chapter you should:

- **understand the origins and outcome of the dyslexia-friendly schools initiative and where you fit into it;**
- **be able to fit the ideas and strategies presented earlier in the book into the context of the dyslexia-friendly school;**
- **have developed ways of evaluating the extent to which your classroom and school is dyslexia-friendly;**
- **have decided how far you might be able to make a difference.**

This chapter addresses the following Professional Standards for QTS and Core:

Q2, C2

Introduction

At the end of this book we return to where we started – the dyslexia-friendly school. Our aim has been to help you to welcome into your classroom vulnerable learners with the differences associated with SpLD/dyslexia and to acknowledge and support these differences in ways that will benefit everyone. We have explored many dimensions of SpLD/dyslexia and prompted you to consider in what ways your classroom and your subject might, without adjustments, present barriers to these potentially talented learners. We have also asked you to look beyond your own practice and the individual child and to see yourself as part of a co-operating team of individuals, both within and beyond the boundaries of the school, who should be united in their goal of adjusting the mainstream setting to make it 'friendly' for all members of the learning and teaching community.

Why 'dyslexia-friendly'?

By now you should have a clear picture of what 'dyslexia–friendly' means to you. Think for a minute and sum up your conclusions in the box below. Do your colleagues and mentor agree?

> **REFLECTIVE TASK**
>
> A dyslexia-friendly school
>
> | Should... | Should not... |
> |---|---|
> | | |

This is your current vision, however you may not be clear about where the concept and principles of *dyslexia-friendly schools* originated or how it has been applied across policy to enable it to work out in practice. We have already established that the idea of the dyslexia-friendly school is closely tied up with changing attitudes to disability, SpLD/dyslexia and inclusion and with the move from the medical 'victim-curing' model of disability to the social 'barrier-breaking' model. But why 'dyslexia-friendly' and where did the initiative originate?

For this we have to look to Swansea Local Authority in 1997 (BDA, 1999). At that point the authority was facing a crisis in its provisions for SpLD/dyslexia. The model in place was a medical one where struggling learners had to await assessment and identification by LA specialists before receiving a Statement entitling them to specialist provision. Insufficient provision to meet needs then resulted in further delays, further frustration for parents, children and schools alike and money spent upon costly tribunals rather than on rectifying the shortage of specialist teachers which would have increased provision for all.

Neil Mackay, who coined the term 'dyslexia-friendly', worked with the SEN adviser Cliff Warwick to overhaul the system. An experimental initiative set up a well resourced and staffed specialist dyslexia unit within one mainstream secondary school and placed the authority's most vulnerable dyslexic students in the school. The emphasis was firmly upon mainstream classrooms and teachers being supported by specialists to take responsibility for these vulnerable learners in an inclusive setting. The outcomes were very positive. GCSE success rates and parental confidence in the school rose markedly and the number of Tribunals and Statements requested for dyslexia dropped. Swansea then instigated awareness training across its schools and initiated accredited training courses in SpLD for teachers and TAs. Mackay worked with a group of SENCos from schools across Wales and England to draw up draft criteria for the 'dyslexia-friendly' school which later became the basis for a national kite-marking scheme to accredit LAs. A local authority will apply for registration on to the scheme and then has two years to show that it has met dyslexia-friendly standards established by the BDA (see www.bda.org.uk). These cover four areas.

- Leadership and management.
- Teaching and learning.
- The classroom environment.
- Partnership and liaison with parents, governors and other concerned parties.

In the autumn of 2007 the Inclusion Development Programme (IDP) was launched. This sets a four-year target for the development and delivery of a programme of Continuing Professional Development (CPD) designed to strengthen the skills and confidence of teachers across mainstream schools in delivering the kind of inclusive practice that will support learners with SEN. The 2007–2008 focus is upon dyslexia and speech, language and communication needs (SLCN) and leading specialist organisations such as Dyslexia Action, the BDA, Patoss, Xtraordinary People and the Helen Arkell Centre are co-operating with the Department for Children, Schools and Families (DCSF) to develop CPD programmes and supporting materials, due to be in schools and Initial Teacher Training from Spring 2008.

To date a range of LAs have achieved the BDA dyslexia-friendly kitemark, or are in the process of doing so, and there have been marked improvements in the experiences of students with SpLD/dyslexia and a shift in attitudes to dyslexia and the ways in which learners might be included. However, Pavey (2007) suggests that, although the majority of LAs now show awareness of the existence of this path, not all are interpreting and following it to the standard envisaged by the BDA. She presents a number of dilemmas including issues of resourcing, the fear that the expertise of central support teams will be lost and disagreement among parents as to whether they would prefer all staff to have a basic knowledge or a few to be experts. Some authorities also question the way in which the dyslexia-friendly school initiative focuses attention and resources upon dyslexia rather than any other need. There also remains no standard model of arrangements for SEN across authorities. Criteria for funding, modes of assessment, administration and teaching vary considerably across county borders. For example, when deciding at what level support might be implemented, some authorities use curriculum levels, others use reading or spelling ages, some require a learner to be in the second percentile (bottom two percent), others only the first and these criteria are not easily obtainable. Try looking on your own Local Authority website to see what information is offered there. If you are interested in pursuing this further, you should refer to Pavey's work (2007).

The dyslexia-friendly 'hierarchy' – where do you fit in?

The story of the development of the dyslexia-friendly initiative and its adoption by LAs makes it clear that it is conceived as firmly based within a top-down policy drive approach, implemented across an authority and involving stakeholders at all levels and in all areas. It is concerned with changing attitudes to managing SpLD/dyslexia and with encouraging the confidence of mainstream teachers to adapt and apply their existing skills (Pavey, 2007). It has implications for resources and training at all levels and, since resources usually stem from local authorities, if the model were expressed as a hierarchy, it could look like this.

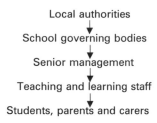

Local authorities
↓
School governing bodies
↓
Senior management
↓
Teaching and learning staff
↓
Students, parents and carers

Figure 11.1 The dyslexia-friendly hierarchy

This is only partly helpful as it places the most important stakeholders at the bottom of the pile with you slightly above. It also leaves out forces that drive change – such as pressure groups, government departments, researchers, academics and trainers. The fact that you are reading this book and aiming to put ideas into practice means that you are likely to be a force for change. Energy sparking from parents, carers and learners themselves frequently means that the impetus comes from 'below'. Co-operation is needed across a range of people to develop the dyslexia-friendly ethos and this teamwork is only likely to increase in line with the emphasis on inter-professional team building promoted through the *Every Child Matters* (2003) agenda. These additional factors suggest that a cycle with interconnecting arrows may be a more appropriate model to illustrate the forces at work.

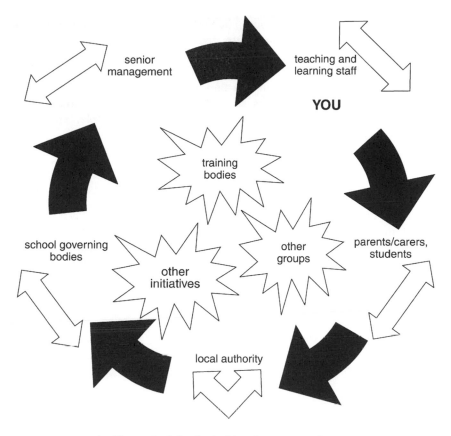

Figure 11.2 Dyslexia-friendly co-operation

This also reminds us that we all have a part to play in creating change. You are maybe at a stage in your career where you are unlikely to feel that you want to get involved at a local authority level, or need to know about the policies in detail, but you should not underestimate the effect on others of your own initiatives in developing your dyslexia-friendly classroom.

MacKay (2004) suggests that there are five key areas in which change must be both fostered and audited to enable a whole school approach.

1. **Policy – putting policy into practice** This is what a school actually does rather than what is written down; what is both written and done: what is written and not done: what is done and not yet written; what is not yet written and needs to be done. Action must be driven by need and discussion. **What does your school policy document say about dyslexia-friendly schools? Do you know anything about the Governing Body and role of the SEN Governor?**
2. **Training – walking the Walk** There is a need for a suitably qualified person to be in a place of influence, and also for whole school awareness, training and catch up programmes. Senior management needs to be seen to be involved. **What training and expertise is offered in your school? Can you find evidence of awareness amongst a range of staff?**
3. **Identification, assessment and monitoring – scrutiny and immediate intervention** This will need to be clearly evident in such practices as classroom teachers feeling able

to flag up individuals and obtain appropriate support and in making policies. **Are these practices current in your school? Are they supported and initiated by senior management?**

4. **Responses to needs – walking the walk**. Dyslexia-friendly practice needs to be evident in all areas of the curriculum. **Can you find examples in your school of alternative assessment methods, easy access to within or out of class support if needed, creative approaches to students' difficulties with, for example, mathematics or foreign languages?**

5. **Parents as partners – completing the loop. What evidence of partnership between parents/carers and the school can you find?**

This type of reflection takes you some way along the path towards evaluating the stage in the dyslexia-friendly process that you and your school have reached. It is, of course, likely that, as with inclusion, different individuals within an institution may be at different points along the road. Pavey (2007) provides detailed self-evaluation/audit tools to help a primary school teacher to evaluate his or her teaching, classroom and school setting. Mackay (2004) also developed an audit checklist based on his five key areas. By now, you should have a clear idea of what to look for and could construct such a tool for yourself.

PRACTICAL TASK PRACTICAL TASK **PRACTICAL TASK** PRACTICAL TASK **PRACTICAL TASK**

Focus on Mackay's key areas 3 and 4. Look back at the summaries for the relevant chapters of this book and draw up a list of criteria that you would look for in a dyslexia-friendly school. Appendix 7 provides you with some help.

> 3: Identification, assessement and monitoring
>
>
>
> 4: Responses to needs

A SUMMARY OF **KEY POINTS**

This final chapter has required you to review the range of needs, strategies and people that the book has presented and to place them within the 'big picture' of the policies which inform the way in which the dyslexia-friendly schools initiative has been implemented in practice. Although there have been many positive changes over the ten years since the term was first coined, there is still much to be done and many contexts in which dyslexia awareness remains lower than it should be. As a new teacher, you can help to make a real difference to learners with SpLD/dyslexia by using these suggestions to make your surroundings truly dyslexia-friendly.

MOVING *ON* > > > > > > MOVING *ON* > > > > > > MOVING *ON*

Can you make a difference?

You may feel that you are very low in the pecking order at present, however, think about the part you might play in the process. By now, you should have a clear picture of what a dyslexia-friendly classroom might look like and some idea as to how far down the road you are. You also know of the existence of a range of resources such as the BDA Dyslexia-friendly Schools pack (2005). Look back at Part 2 and consider the adjustments you might be making in your classroom. Consider the following six elements and list for each a couple of changes you could make in the way you operate.

PRACTICAL TASK PRACTICAL TASK **PRACTICAL TASK** PRACTICAL TASK **PRACTICAL TASK**

Your students

Your classroom assistants

Parent/carers

Your classroom layout

Your subject

Your resources

Share these ideas with your colleagues between and within schools, your mentor, your TA, even your students. You will be pleasantly surprised at the speed with which your resources and strategies multiply. If you are not currently doing these things, there will come a time in the future when you will be able to draw breath and do so and ensure that you remain a dyslexia-friendly teacher.

FURTHER READING FURTHER READING FURTHER READING FURTHER READING

British Dyslexia Association (BDA) (2005) *Achieving dyslexia-friendly schools*. (5th edition). Reading: BDA. Available online at www.bdaweb.co.uk/bda/downloads/wholedocument.pdf

Mackay, N and Tresman, S (2006) *Achieving dyslexia-friendly schools*. Oxford: SEN Marketing.

Pavey, B (2007) *The dyslexia-friendly primary school*. London: Paul Chapman Publishing.

Reid, G (2005) *Dyslexia and inclusion. Classroom approaches for assessment, teaching and learning*. London: David Fulton.

DfES (2002) *Learning and teaching for dyslexic children*. www.standards.dfes.gov.uk CD-Rom available.

Appendix 1
Definitions of dyslexia – Which one would you choose?

1. World Federation of Neurologists (1968, cited by Reid, 1995, p2).
Dyslexia is a disorder manifested by difficulty in learning to read despite conventional instruction and sociocultural opportunity. It is dependent upon fundamental cognitive disabilities which are frequently of constitutional origin.

2. World Federation of Neurology (1968)
A disorder in children who, despite conventional classroom experience, fail to attain the language skills of reading, writing and spelling commensurate with their intellectual abilities. (Waites, 1968)

3. Dyslexia Institute (1989)
Specific Learning Difficulties can be defined as organising or learning deficiencies which restrict the students' competencies in information processing, in motor skills and working memory, so causing limitations in some or all of the skills of speech, reading, spelling, writing, essay writing, numeracy and behaviour.

4. British Dyslexia Association: 1996
Dyslexia: *... is a complex **neurological** condition which is constitutional in origin. The symptoms may affect many areas of learning and function, and may be described as a specific difficulty in reading, spelling and written language. One or more of these areas may be affected. Numeracy, notational skills (music), motor function and organisational skills may also be involved. However, it is particularly related to mastering written language, although oral language may be affected to some degree.* (Crisfield, 1996)

5. National Working Party for Dyslexia in Higher Education (NWPDHE, 1999)
Dyslexia is a neurological condition which is characterised by a variety of cognitive impairments or neurological anomalies. Individuals with dyslexia typically manifest problems in areas such as phonological processing, memory (especially short-term or working memory), visual perception (e.g. visual discomfort) and motor co-ordination (dyspraxia). Difficulties in these areas will not necessarily all be seen in the same individual with dyslexia, but if no difficulty in any of these areas can be detected then a diagnosis of dyslexia must be regarded with suspicion.

6. Frith, U (2002) Neuro-cognitive framework, Researcher
The consensus is emerging that dyslexia is a neuro-developmental disorder with a biological origin which impacts on speech processing with a range of clinical manifestations. There is evidence for a genetic basis and there is evidence for a brain basis, and it is clear that the behavioural signs extend well beyond written language. There may be many different kinds of genes and different kinds of brain conditions that are ultimately responsible for the dyslexia syndrome, but, in each case the symptoms have to be understood within the relevant cultural context.

7. Siegel and Smythe (2004) Researchers in the field of SpLD/dyslexia and multilingualism
Dyslexia is a difficulty in the acquisition of literacy skills that is neurological in origin. It is evident when accurate and fluent word reading, spelling and writing develop very incompletely or with great difficulty. This does not negate the existence of co-morbid difficulties including receptive and expressive oral language deficits, visual and auditory system deficits, developmental co-ordination difficulties and dyscalculia.

8. British Psychological Society (1999 p18) Educational Psychologists
Dyslexia: *... is evident when accurate and fluent word reading and/or spelling develops very incompletely or with great difficulty.*

9. British Dyslexia Association (quoted by Peer, 2001, p11)
Dyslexia is *a combination of abilities and difficulties that affect the learning process in one or more of reading, spelling and writing. Accompanying weaknesses may be identified in areas of speed of processing, short-term memory, sequencing, auditory and/or visual perception, spoken language and motor skills. It is particularly related to mastering and using written language which may include alphabetic, numeric and musical notation*

10. Dyslexia Action (formerly Dyslexia Institute) 25.07.2007
Dyslexia is a specific learning difficulty that mainly affects reading and spelling. Dyslexia is characterised by difficulties in processing word-sounds and by weaknesses in short-term verbal memory; its effects may be seen in spoken language as well as written language. The current evidence suggests that these difficulties arise from inefficiencies in language-processing areas in the left hemisphere of the brain which, in turn, appear to be linked to genetic differences.

Dyslexia is life-long, but its effects can be minimised by targeted literacy intervention, technological support and adaptations to ways of working and learning. Dyslexia is not related to intelligence, race or social background. Dyslexia varies in severity and often occurs alongside other specific learning difficulties, such as Dyspraxia or Attention Deficit Disorder, resulting in variation in the degree and nature of individuals' strengths and weaknesses.

SpLD/ Dyslexia statement	T/M/S
1. The majority of dyslexic learners are male.	M
2. Dyslexic individuals are usually good at art.	S
3. Dyslexic learners will never learn to read.	M
4. Dyslexia runs in families.	T
5. Dyslexia does not exist in other languages.	M
6. Dyslexic learners have difficulty with maths.	S
7. Most dyslexic learners suffer from attention disorders.	M
8. All dyslexic individuals are disorganised.	S
9. Dyslexic individuals are usually good at sport.	S
10. Dyslexic learners need to put extra effort into their school work.	T
11. Dyslexic children have difficulty concentrating.	S
12. Dyslexic learners are articulate.	S
13. Dyslexic children often have difficulties with their peer group.	S
14. Dyslexic learners have low self-esteem.	S
15. Many dyslexic learners have difficulty with alphabetical order.	T
16. It is impossible to identify dyslexia before the age of 7.	M
17. Children with and without dyslexia use different brain areas for language tasks.	T
18. Dyslexic learners are highly creative.	S
19. Dyslexic students find it hard to express themselves in writing.	T
20. Dyslexia does not exist.	M
21. All dyslexic learners are of average or above average intelligence.	M
22. Dyslexic learners cannot cope at university.	M
23. Dyslexic children are impulsive.	S
24. Dyslexic learners have trouble listening to information.	S
25. There is more than one type of dyslexia.	T
26. Dyslexic learners are all likely to have right-brain thought characteristics.	S
27. Dyslexic learners have trouble with eye-strain.	S
28. Dyslexic learners have difficulty with short-term memory.	T
29. Dyslexic learners are clumsy.	S
30. Dyslexic learners have persistent difficulties with spelling.	T
31. Dyslexic learners have trouble with lists and sequences.	T
32. Dyslexic learners have trouble focussing on more than one activity at a time.	S
33. Dyslexic learners find it hard to make skills automatic.	T
34. Dyslexic learners suffer from early language delay.	S
35. Dyslexic learners have more difficulty than most with taking notes.	T
36. Dyslexic learners find it hard to copy from a board.	T
37. Dyslexic learners have poor letter formation and written presentation.	S
38. Dyslexic learners have difficulty with articulation.	S
39. A dyslexic learner will be the class clown.	S
40. Dyslexic learners produce mirror writing.	S
41. Dyslexic adults will read slowly and laboriously.	T
42. Dyslexic learners are usually left-handed.	S
43. Dyslexic learners have low reading ages and high IQs.	S
44. Dyslexic learners come from middle-class families.	M

Appendix 2
Checking readability of a text using Word

Create **Word** document containing text to be checked.

1. Go to **Tools**
2. Then **Options**
3. Then **Spelling and Grammar**
4. Place tick in box next to **Readability Statistics**
5. Click **OK** and close screen.

Run the spellchecker over the required document. When complete, the screen will display **readability statistics**. Check **Fleisch–Kincaid** level (American grades) and add 5 to get reading age of text. The higher the number of passive sentences, the higher the reading age.

Adapted from Pavey, 2007

Appendix 3
One example of a time line

Events in *Of Mice and Men*

Day	Time	Place	People	Events
Friday	Evening	By the river	George, Lennie	Camp near ranch before job. Dream of owning land. G looks after L
Saturday	Morning	Ranch bunk house	L, L, Candy, Boss, Curley, C's wife	Meet others. G tells L to keep away from Curley's wife
Saturday	Early evening	Bunk house	Candy, G, L, Carlson, Slim, Curley, etc.	Carlson shoots Candy's dog, makes G and L's dream possible. Curley attacks L. Fist crushed
Saturday	Night	Crook's room	Crook, L, Candy, Curley's wife, G	L visits Crook. Talk about land and loneliness. Crook offers to join dream but humiliated by C's wife
Sunday	Afternoon	The barn	C's wife, L, later G, Candy	L kills his puppy then C's wife. Manhunt starts
Sunday	Later	By the river	L, G, later Slim, Curley and others	G shoots L to save him from Curley

Reproduced from Mortimore (2008)

A time-line can also be laid out horizontally – it depends on the nature of the information. You will need to experiment.

Appendix 4
Situation, Problem, Solution, Outcome (SPSO)

The basic links of a story, set of events or even a science experiment can be shown as follows.

- Situation
- Problem
- Solution
- Outcome

Students can be shown how to use this to analyse text or create their own.

1. Start by telling any simple story, for example, from the start of Macbeth:
   It is the day after the battle. Macbeth and Banquo are returning home when they meet three witches. They tell Macbeth that he will become King. He is both appalled and tempted by this. What will he do?
2. Stop here, ask the group to suggest what Macbeth should do.
3. While the group are thinking/discussing, write on the board:

Situation	Witches foretell that Macbeth will become King.
Problem	How can he achieve this legally?
Solution	
Outcome	

4. Ask for the solutions to Macbeth's problem and add some to the chart. e.g.

Situation	Witches foretell that Macbeth will become King.
Problem	How can he achieve this legally?
Solution	He consults his wife.
Outcome	She suggests he might murder the king.
Final outcome	

As indicated by the arrow, this may involve a number of SPSOs prior to reaching the final outcome.

This can also be used in other curriculum areas as shown:

History
Situation Japan wanted to invade Southeast Asia.
Problem The American fleet posed a threat
Solution The Japanese Air Force bombed Pearl Harbour
Outcome After this they moved into the areas they wanted.

Chemistry
Situation Two solids, sugar and sand, are mixed.
Problem How can they be separated?
Solution Place them in water.
Outcome One dissolves in the water, and the other does not. This therefore separates the two substances.

Appendix 5
The BUG technique

Developed by Dr Geraldine Price, Southampton University (2006).

Look carefully at the question:

Evaluate the impact of the growth of Fascism upon German society in the years immediately preceding the outbreak of World War II.

The student then **BOXES (B)** the word which gives the **type** of answer required.

⟦Evaluate⟧ **the impact of the growth of Fascism upon German society in the years immediately preceding the outbreak of World War II**.

The student then **UNDERLINES (U)** the keywords needed for the answer.

⟦Evaluate⟧ **the** <u>impact</u> of the <u>growth of Fascism</u> upon <u>German society</u> in the <u>years immediately preceding the outbreak of World War II</u>.

The student then **GLANCES (G)** back to ensure that all the necessary key words are included.

BUG

The student then needs to ensure that he/she has understood the implications of the boxed word (Evaluate) and the meanings of the subject specific vocabulary. Information can then be attached to the key words and an answer/essay built around them. This approach has been found helpful with a range of humanities subjects where extended writing may be required either within an exam situation or for course work. It has also been found to be a useful way of helping students interpret maths examination questions and make links between the language and the calculations required.

Appendix 6
Conflict prevention chart

Type of difficulty	Situation	Problem	People involved student and ...	Possible solutions
Reading				
Spelling				
Phonological difficulties				
Written expression				
Organisation				
Memory				
Automaticity				
Speed of processing				
Sequencing				

Appendix 7
Dyslexia-friendly schools

Audit Checklist

Adapted from Mackay (2004)

3. Identification, assessment and monitoring

Criteria	Date/In place? What?	Action needed	Second check
Documented ways of identifying issues with regard to basic skill development			
Classroom based intervention strategies			
Needs-assessment processes in place			
Dyslexia-friendly marking systems			
Dyslexia-friendly testing assessment			

4: Responses to needs

Criteria	Date/In place? What?	Action needed	Second check
Good practice in policies			
Classroom management strategies in staff handbook			
Information about students fully available			
Dyslexia-friendly materials used by all staff			
Dyslexia-friendly testing and marking systems used by all staff			
Dyslexia-friendly homework practices			
Work acceptable in range of forms			
Strategies in place to access material for exam revision and research			
Strategies in place to compensate for poor literary skills			

References

Ainscow, M (2000) The Next step for special education. Supporting the development of inclusive practices. *British Journal of Special Education*, 27, 2, 76–80

Backhouse, G and Morris, K (2005) *Dyslexia: Assessing and reporting*. The Patoss Guide. London: Patoss

Barton, L (ed.) (1996) *Disability and society: Emerging issues and insights*. Harlow: Addison Wesley Longman

BDA (1999) *Promoting dyslexia-friendly schools*. www.bdadyslexia.org.uk/pictures/promoting school.pdf

BDA (2006) *Achieving dyslexia-friendly schools resource pack*. 5th edition. Reading: BDA www.bdadyslexia.org.uk

Blakemore, S and Frith, U (2005) *The Learning brain: Lessons for education*. Oxford: Blackwell

Booth, T and Ainscow, M (2002) *Index for inclusion: Developing learning and participation in schools*. Bristol: Centre for Studies in Inclusive Education (CSIE)

Bruck, M (1990) Word recognition skills of adults with childhood diagnoses of dyslexia. *Developmental Psychology*, 26, 439–54

Bruck, M (1992) Persistence of dyslexics' phonological awareness deficits. *Developmental Psychology*, 28, 74–86

Burden, B (2005) *Dyslexia and self-concept*. London: Whurr Publishers

Butterworth, B (1999) *The mathematical brain*. London: Macmillan

Butterworth, B (2003) *Dyscalculia screener*. Windsor: nferNelson

Butterworth, B and Yeo, D (2004) *Dyscalculia guidance*. Windsor: nferNelson

Buzan, T (1982) *Use your head*, London: BBC Books

Calderdale Education Authority (2004) *Promoting inclusion: Dyslexia-friendly schools*. Available from www.thebdashop.org

Chasty, H (1985) What is dyslexia? In Snowling, M J (ed.) *Children's written language difficulties*. Windsor: nferNelson

Chinn, S (2004) *The Trouble with maths. A practical guide to helping learners with numeracy difficulties*. Abingdon: Routledge

Chinn, S and Ashcroft, T (1998) *Mathematics for dyslexics: A teaching handbook*. London: Whurr Publishers

Clausen-May, T (2005) *Teaching maths to pupils with different learning styles*. London: Paul Chapman Publishing

Coffield, F, Moseley, D, Hall, E and Ecclestone, K (2004) *Should we be using learning styles? What research has to say to practitioners*. Learning and Skills Development Agency (LSDA) http://www.LSDA.org.uk

Cogan, J and Flecker, M (2004) *Dyslexia in the secondary school. A practical handbook for teachers, parents and students*. London: Whurr Publishers

Coleman, R and Buzan, T (1999) *Teach yourself literature guides*. London: Hodder & Stoughton

Critchley, M (1970) *The Dyslexic child*. London: Heinemann

Crombie, M and McColl, H (2001) Dyslexia and the teaching of modern foreign languages. In Peer, L and Reid, G (eds) *Dyslexia: Successful inclusion in the secondary school*. London: David Fulton

Dargie, R (2001) Dyslexia and history. In Peer, L and Reid, G (eds) *Dyslexia: Successful inclusion in the secondary school*. London: David Fulton

Denckla, M B and Rudel, R G (1976) Rapid 'Automatized' Naming (RAN) Dyslexia differentiates from other learning disabilities. *Neuropsychologia*, 14, 471–9

Department for Education and Employment (2001) *Key Stage 3 National Strategy*. London: DfEE

Department for Education and Skills (2001) *Special Educational Needs: Code of Practice of Schools, Early Education Practitioners and other interested parties*. Date of Issue: November 2001 Ref: DfES/581/2001 Special Educational Needs Code of Practice

Department of Education (1994) *Code of Practice on the Identification and Assessment of Special Educational Needs*. London: Department of Education

Deponio, P (2004) The Co-occurrence of specific learning difficulties: implications for identification and assessment. In Reid, G and Fawcett, A (eds) *Dyslexia in context*. London: Whurr Publishers

DfEE (2000) *Working with teaching assistants: A Good practice guide* (ref: DfES 0148/2000)

DfES (2001) *Guidance to support pupils with dyslexia and dyscalculia.* National Numeracy Strategy

Ditchfield, D (2001) Dyslexia and music. In Peer, L and Reid, G (eds) (2001) *Dyslexia – Successful inclusion in the secondary school*. London: David Fulton

Dore, W (2007) *Developing skills for life* (www.DDAT.co.uk)

Downey, D and Snyder, L (1999) *College students with dyslexia, persistent linguistic deficits and foreign learning. Paper* – Manchester: BDA Conference on Multilingualism and Dyslexia

Dunn, R and Dunn, K (1991) *Teaching students through their individual learning styles. A practical approach*. Needham Heights, MA: Allyn & Bacon

Dupree, J (2005) *Help students improve their study skills*. London: David Fulton

Dyslexia Action (2007) www.dyslexiaaction.co.uk

Edwards, J (1994) *The Scars of dyslexia: Eight case studies in emotional reactions*. London: Cassell

Elliott, J (2005) *The Death of dyslexia conference*. London: November 2005

Fawcett, A J (ed.) (2001) *Dyslexia: Theory and good practice*. London: Whurr Publishers

Fawcett, A J (2004) Dyslexia: *From theory to practice*. Keynote Speech Presented at BDA International Conference. Warwick University

Fawcett, A and Nicolson, R (1996) *Dyslexia screening test (DST)*. London: The Psychological Corporation/Harcourt Brace and Company

Frith, U (1985) Beneath the surface of developmental dyslexia. In Marshall, J, Patterson, K and Coltheart, M (eds) *Surface Dyslexia*. Abingdon: Routledge & Kegan Paul

Frith, U (1997) Brain, mind and behaviours in dyslexia. In Hulme, C and Snowling, M (eds) *Dyslexia: Biology, cognition and intervention.* London: Whurr Publishers

Frith, U (1999) Paradoxes in the definition of dyslexia. *Dyslexia: An International Journal of Research & Practice*, 5 (4), 192–214

Frith, U (2002) Resolving the Paradoxes of Dyslexia. In Reid, G and Wearmouth, J (eds) *Dyslexia and literacy*. Chichester: Wiley

Gardner, H (1983) *Frames of mind*. New York: Basic Books

Gough, P and Tunmer, W (1986) Decoding, reading and reading disability. *Remedial and Special Education*, 7, 6–10

Griffiths, M (2002) *Study skills and dyslexia in the secondary school: A practical approach*. London: David Fulton

Hales, G (2004) *Chickens and eggs. The Effects of the erosion of self-esteem and self-images by treating outcomes as causes*. Paper presented at The Sixth BDA International Conference. University of Warwick. Reading: BDA

Hatcher, J and Snowling, M (2002) The Phonological representations hypothesis of dyslexia. In Reid, G and Wearmouth, J (eds) *Dyslexia and literacy: Theory and practice*. Chichester: Wiley

Henderson A (1998) *Maths for the dyslexic: A Practical guide*. 2nd edition. London: David Fulton

Humphrey, N and Mullins, P (2002b) Self-Concept and self-esteem in developmental dyslexia. *Journal of Research in Special Educational Needs*, 2 (2), www.nasen.uk.com

Hunter,V (2001) Dyslexia and general science. In Peer, L and Reid, G (eds) *Dyslexia: Successful inclusion in the secondary school*. London: David Fulton

Johnson, M (2004) Dyslexia-friendly teaching. In Thomson, M (ed.) *Dyslexia: Perspectives for classroom practitioners.* Reading: BDA

Kay, J and Yeo, D (2003) *Dyslexia and maths*. London: David Fulton

Klein, C (1995) *Diagnosing dyslexia*. London: Adult Literacy and Basic Skills Unit

Knight, D and Hynd, G (2002) The Neurobiology of dyslexia. In Reid, G and Wearmouth, J (eds) *Dyslexia and literacy*. Chichester: Wiley

Long, R (2007) *The Rob Long Omnibus edition of better behaviour*. London: David Fulton/NASEN

MacKay, N (2004) The Case for dyslexia-friendly schools. In Reid, G and Fawcett, A (eds) *Dyslexia in context. Research, policy and practice*. London: Whurr Publishers

Margerison, A (1997) Class teachers and the role of the classroom assistants in the delivery of special education. *Support for Learning*, 12, 4, 166–9

McColl, H (2000) *Modern languages for all*. London: David Fulton

Miles, T R (1983) *Dyslexia: The Pattern of difficulties.* London: Collins

Miles, T R (1993) Dyslexia: *The Pattern of difficulties*. 2nd edition. London: Whurr Publishers

Miles, T R and Gilroy, D (1986) *Dyslexia at college*. London: Methuen

Miles, T R; Wheeler, T J and Haslum, M N (1998) Gender ratio in dyslexia. *Annals of dyslexia*, 68, 27–55

Mortimore, T (2003) *Dyslexia and learning style. A practitioner's handbook*. London: Whurr Publishers

Mortimore, T (2006) *The Impact of dyslexia and cognitive style upon the study skills and experience of students in higher education*. Cardiff University: Unpublished Doctoral Dissertation

Mortimore, T (2008) *Dyslexia and learning style. A practitioner's handbook*. 2nd edition. Chichester: Wiley

Mortimore, T and Crozier, W R (2006) Dyslexia and difficulties with study skills in higher education. *Studies in Higher Education*, 31, 2, 235–51

Nicolson, R and Fawcett, A (1994) Comparison of Deficits in Cognitive and Motor Skills in Children with Dyslexia. *Annals of Dyslexia*, 44, 147–64

Nicolson, R I (2002) The Dyslexia Ecosystem. *Dyslexia: An International Journal of Research and Practice*, 8, 55–66

Nind, M (2005) Models and practice in inclusive curricula. In Nind, M, Rix, J, Sheehy, K and Simmons, K (eds) *Curriculum and pedagogy in inclusive education. Values into practice*. Abingdon: Routledge Falmer

Oliver, M (1990) *The Politics of disablement*. Basingstoke: Macmillan

Ott, P (1997) *How to detect and manage dyslexia*. Oxford: Heinemann

Ott, P (2007) *Teaching children with dyslexia. A practical guide*. Abingdon: Routledge

Parsons, R (ed.) (1997) *GCSE: Double science: Biology. The Revision guide higher level*. Cumbria: Coordination Group Publications www.cgpboopks.co.uk

Pavey, B (2007) *The Dyslexia-friendly primary school*. London: Paul Chapman Publishing

Peer, L (2004) United Kingdom Policy for Inclusion. In Reid, G and Fawcett, A (eds) *Dyslexia in context. Research, policy and practice*. London: Whurr Publishers

Peer, L and Reid, G (eds) (2000) *Multilingualism, literacy and dyslexia: A challenge for educators*. London: David Fulton

Peer, L and Reid, G (2001) *Dyslexia: Successful inclusion in the secondary school*. London: David Fulton

Pickering, S J (2004) Verbal Memory in the Learning of Literacy. In Turner, M and Rack, J (eds) *The Study of dyslexia*. New York: Kluwer Academic /Plenum

Pollock, J, Waller, E and Politt, R (2004) *Day-to-day dyslexia in the classroom*. 2nd edition. Abingdon: RoutledgeFalmer

Price, G (2006) Lecture within the inclusive learning environments module of the MSc in SpLD/ dyslexia. Southampton University

Price, G A (2007) Inclusion: Special educational needs. In Ellis, V (ed.). *Learning and teaching in secondary schools*. 2nd edition. Exeter: Learning Matters

Pumfrey, P and Reason, R (1998) *Specific learning difficulties (Dyslexia): Challenges and responses*. Abingdon: Routledge

Rack, J (1994) Dyslexia: The Phonological deficit hypothesis. In Nicolson, R and Fawcett, A (eds) *Dyslexia in children: Multidisciplinary perspectives*. Hemel Hempstead: Harvester Wheatsheaf

Reid, G (2005) *Dyslexia and inclusion. Classroom approaches for assessment, teaching and learning*. London: David Fulton

Reid, G (2003) *Dyslexia: A practitioner's handbook*. 3rd edition. Chichester: Wiley

Reid, G (2005a) *Learning styles and inclusion*. London: Paul Chapman Publishing

Reid, G (2006) *Dyslexia*. The SEN Series. London: Continuum

Reid, G and Wearmouth, J (eds) (2002) *Dyslexia and literacy*. Chichester: Wiley.

Rice, M and Brooks, G (2004) *Developmental dyslexia in adults: A research review*. London: NRDC

Riddick, B (1996) *Living with dyslexia*. Abingdon: Routledge

Riding, R and Rayner, S (1998) *Cognitive styles and learning strategies*. London: David Fulton

Robertson, J (2000) *Dyslexia and reading: A Neuropsychological approach*. London: Whurr Publishers

Robertson, J and Bakker, D (2002) The Balance model of reading and dyslexia. In Reid G and Wearmouth J (eds) *Dyslexia and literacy. Theory and practice*. Chichester: Wiley

Robson, P (2001) *Maths dictionary*. 2nd edition. Scarborough: Newby Books

Scott, R (2004) *Dyslexia and counselling*. London: Whurr Publishers

Seligman, M P (1990) *Learned optimism*. New York: Pocket Books

Shaywitz, S, Shaywitz, B, Fletcher, J and Escobar, M (1990) Prevalence of reading disorders in boys and girls: Results of the Connecticut longitudinal study. *Journal of the American Medical Association*, 264, 998–1002

Singleton, C (1999) *Dyslexia in higher education: policy, provision and practice. Report of the National Working Party on Dyslexia in Higher Education*. HEFCE and University of Hull

Snowling, M (1987) *Dyslexia: A Cognitive developmental perspective*. Oxford: Blackwell

Snowling, M (2000) *Dyslexia*. 2nd edition. Oxford: Blackwell

Snowling, M and Hulme, C (1994) The Development of phonological skills in children. *Philosophical transactions of The Royal Society of London*. B346, 21–28. UK: Athenaeum

Snowling, M and Stackhouse, J (2006) Dyslexia, speech and language. 2nd edition. London: Whurr Publishers

Soan, S (2005) A*chieving QTS: Reflective reader. Primary special educational needs*. Exeter: Learning Matters

Stanovich, K (1988) Explaining the differences between the dyslexic and the garden-variety poor reader: The Phonological-core variable-difference model. *Journal of Learning Disabilities*, 21, (10) 590–604

Stanovich, K (1996) Towards a more inclusive definition of dyslexia. *Dyslexia*, 2, 179–89

Stein, J (2004) Dyslexia genetics. In Reid G and Fawcett A (eds) *Dyslexia in context: Research, policy and practice*. London: Whurr Publishers

Stein, J (2007) *Wobbles, warbles and fish. The Magnocellular theory of dyslexia*. Keynote Address. University of Southampton and The Helen Arkell Dyslexia Centre Conference. Practically There. Southampton University

Stein, J and Walsh, V (1997) To see; but not to read; The Magnocellular theory of dyslexia. *TINS* 20, 147–51

Tallal, P (1984) Temporal or phonetic processing deficit in dyslexia? *Applied Psycholinguistics*, 5, (2) 167–9

Thomson, M (2004) Implications for the classroom. In Reid, G and Fawcett, A (eds) *Dyslexia in context: Research, policy and practice*. London: Whurr Publishers

Thomson, M and Chinn, S (2001) Good practice in secondary school. In Fawcett, A (ed.) *Dyslexia: theory and good practice*. London: Whurr Publishers

Thomson, M (ed.) (2004) *Dyslexia: Perspectives for classroom practitioners*. Reading: BDA

Townend, J and Turner, M (2000) *Dyslexia in practice: A Guide for teachers*. New York: Kluwer Academic/Plenum Publishers

Townend, J and Walker, J (2006) *Structure of language: Spoken and written English*. London: Whurr Publishers

Turner, M (1997) *Psychological assessment of dyslexia*. London: Whurr Publishers

Turner, M and Rack, J (2004) *The Study of dyslexia*. New York: Kluwer Academic/Plenum

Wolf, M and Bowers, P G (2000) Naming-speed processes and developmental reading disabilities: An Introduction to the special issue on the double-deficit hypothesis. *Journal of Learning Disabilities* 33, 322–4

Yeo, D (2003) *Dyslexia, dyspraxia and mathematics*. London: Whurr Publishers

www.bdadyslexia.org.uk

www.bdadyslexia.org.uk/pictures/promotingschool.pdf

www.cgpboopks.co.uk

www.DDAT.co.uk

www.dyslexiaaction.co.uk

www.literacytrust.org.uk/campaign/SMOG.html

www.LSDA.org.uk

www.nasen.uk.com

www.nasen.uk.comwww.teachernet.gov.uk/*wholeschool/sen/senglossary/* (2008)

www.thebdashop.org

www.warwick.ac.uk/staff/D.J.Wray/index.html